ALL THIS MARVELOUS POTENTIAL

ROBERT KENNEDY'S 1968 TOUR OF APPALACHIA

MATTHEW ALGEO

Published by Chicago Review Press Incorporated
814 North Franklin Street
Chicago, Illinois 60610
ISBN 978-1-64160-059-0

Poem "The Dreamer" courtesy of Lawrence Baldridge.

Portions of chapter 9 have previously appeared, in substantially different form, as an article in the online magazine *We're History*.

Library of Congress Cataloging-in-Publication Data
Is available from the Library of Congress.

Typesetting: Nord Compo
Map design: Chris Erichsen

Printed in the United States of America
5 4 3 2 1

The Dreamer

by Lawrence Baldridge

He came a light to our mountains.
A young man burdened with personal tragedy,
And pained with a nation's lost direction
In a war that consumed youth, idealism, and a nation's dignity.

He came a light to our mountains,
In a nation divided by class and prejudice;
And had himself championed civil rights for all
Whatever one's class, or creed, or color.

He came a light to our mountains—
On unpaved roads, past humble dwellings, down endless "hollars."
And this Dreamer, this Joseph, found himself inside another dream,
The dream of Alice Lloyd of Boston, our college founder.

He came a light to our mountains
And spoke eloquently and passionately to the students of Alice Lloyd:
And they dreamed with him,
Dreamed of peace among nations, of good will to all mankind.

He came a light to our mountains
And seemed so much at home.
He spoke here, walked here, slept here, ate here.
Robert Kennedy came to Caney Creek!

And the light still shines!

Contents

Part III: Wednesday, February 14, 1968

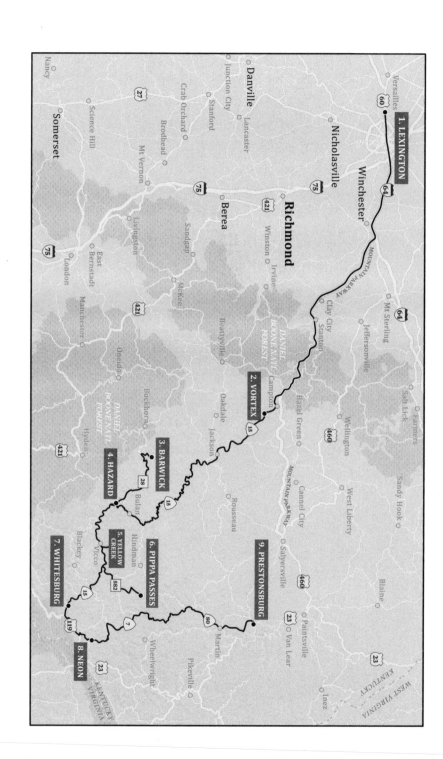

Robert F. Kennedy's Itinerary

All times are approximate.

Tuesday, February 13, 1968

11:00 AM	Arrives at Blue Grass Airport in Lexington on Eastern Airlines Flight 659, is greeted by former Kentucky governor Albert Benjamin "Happy" Chandler.
11:30 AM	Departs the airport in a state-owned vehicle provided by Kentucky's recently elected Republican governor, Louie Nunn. A state trooper is behind the wheel. Riding along are Congressman Carl D. Perkins and Steve Cawood, a University of Kentucky law student. A large caravan of reporters follows.
1:00 PM	Arrives at the one-room schoolhouse in Vortex, Wolfe County, where he convenes a one-man hearing of the Senate Subcommittee on Employment, Manpower, and Poverty. Among those testifying are Swango Fugate, a disabled miner from Breathitt County, and Mary Rice Farris, an African American activist from Madison County.
2:30 PM	Visits poor families in Breathitt and Wolfe Counties; inspects the one-room schoolhouse in Barwick, Breathitt

County, where he meets the teacher, Bonnie Jean Carroll, and her students.

3:30 PM   Tours Liberty Street, the predominantly African American neighborhood in Hazard, Perry County.

5:00 PM   Inspects a strip mine at Yellow Creek, near Vicco, Perry County.

7:00 PM   Arrives at Alice Lloyd College in Pippa Passes, Knott County. Holds a ninety-minute question-and-answer session with approximately two hundred students in the school's auditorium and overnights in the home of one of the college's vice presidents.

Wednesday, February 14, 1968

8:00 AM   Delivers brief remarks on the steps of the Letcher County Courthouse in Whitesburg.

10:00 AM   Convenes a hearing of the Subcommittee on Employment, Manpower, and Poverty in the gymnasium of Fleming-Neon High School in Neon, Letcher County. Among those testifying are Tommy Duff, a senior at Evarts High School in neighboring Harlan County, and David Zegeer, the manager of Bethlehem Steel's mining subsidiary in eastern Kentucky.

1:30 PM   Departs Neon. Visits families in Jackhorn, McRoberts, and Haymond, Kentucky.

4:00 PM   Delivers brief remarks on the steps of the Floyd County Courthouse in Prestonsburg, Kentucky.

4:30 PM   Flies from a small airport near Prestonsburg to Louisville on Governor Nunn's plane.

6:00 PM   Attends a reception in his honor at the home of Mary and Barry Bingham Sr., publishers of the *Louisville Courier-Journal*.

Introduction

THE APPALACHIAN MOUNTAINS WERE FORMED about three billion years ago, when all the continents came together to form a single giant super-continent that geologists call Pangaea.

Somewhere along the Carolina coast, Africa crashed into North America—albeit at a speed so slow as to confound human comprehension—and crumpled the eastern half of what is now the United States. Waves of mountains rose up. Over the ensuing two billion years, the weight of the mountains pressed down on deep layers of dead and decomposing organic matter (mostly prehistoric plants), squeezing out the oxygen and turning the mush into peat, which, after another few hundred million years, turned into a carbon-based black rock that burns slowly and emits tremendous heat: coal.

The Appalachians may have once stood as tall as the Himalayas stand today. Time has worn them down, but they are still formidable. And they are still pressing down, and squeezing, in ways both literal and figurative.

Just over fifty years ago, in February 1968, Robert Kennedy, a US senator born into great wealth and privilege, went to the Appalachian Mountains in eastern Kentucky to meet with people born at the opposite end of the social and economic spectrum: disabled coal miners, single and widowed mothers, children whose parents could not afford to feed them adequately.

The trip occurred at a pivotal moment in American history—the Tet Offensive had launched just weeks before—and at a pivotal moment in Robert Kennedy's life: he was mulling a run for the presidency. For two days, Kennedy traveled hundreds of miles up and down the hills and hollows of eastern Kentucky, on what the press dubbed a "poverty tour." He visited one-room schoolhouses and dilapidated homes. He held a public hearing in a ramshackle high school gymnasium, sitting behind a wooden table set up in the foul lane. He toured a strip mine and spoke at a small mountain college.

As acting chairman of a Senate subcommittee on poverty, Robert Kennedy went to Kentucky to gauge the progress of the War on Poverty launched four years earlier by his brother's successor, Lyndon Johnson.

Robert Kennedy wasn't merely on a fact-finding mission, however; a cold political calculus was at work too. Kennedy was considering challenging President Johnson for the Democratic presidential nomination, but he would need support from white voters to win it. Kennedy's main constituencies were dispossessed minorities: African Americans, Mexican Americans, Native Americans. He needed to forge a coalition between them and working-class whites. "Let's face it," he told a reporter, "I appeal best to people who have problems."

His trip to eastern Kentucky was a dry run for his presidential campaign, an opportunity to test his antiwar and antipoverty message with hardscrabble whites. He was greeted by what one biographer has described as a mixture of adulation and loathing. Young people mobbed him like he was a Beatle, begging him for autographs and tousling his own famous mop top. Their parents, however, were more circumspect. Frustrated by the government's continued inability to improve their lives—and by years of unkept promises—they warned Kennedy of a growing anger toward Washington.

A month after his visit, Kennedy officially announced he was challenging Johnson for the Democratic nomination.

Four months after his visit, he was murdered. He was forty-two. He was survived by his wife, Ethel, and their ten children. Their eleventh child would be born six months after his death.

This is the story of Robert Kennedy's visit to the mountains of eastern Kentucky in the turbulent and chaotic winter of 1967–68, when Vietnam and Peggy Fleming competed for headlines, the Beatles were at the top of the charts (with "Hello, Goodbye"), and the nation's unrest reached deep into Appalachia. It's also the stories of the people Kennedy touched in his brief time there, and how the trip continues to reverberate in their lives and communities, in ways large and small, even all these years later.

Part I

Before the Trip

Robert F. Kennedy in 1968. *Sven Walnum Photograph Collection; John F. Kennedy Presidential Library and Museum*

1

Night

THE COVER OF THE JANUARY 12, 1968, issue of *Life* magazine (price: thirty-five cents) featured Faye Dunaway, costar of one of that winter's most popular and controversial films, *Bonnie and Clyde*, in a long cardigan suit and a 1930s-style beret, an ensemble inspired by the film. "Faye is a perfectionist—and a worrier," the accompanying profile noted. "She won't eat and mostly ignores the glasses of Tab she orders one after another." Far less glamorous was another article in the issue. Titled "These Murdered Old Mountains," it told *Life*'s seven million readers of the devastation wrought by strip mining in eastern Kentucky.

Appalachia had been "discovered" by the mass media five years earlier, when Harry Caudill published *Night Comes to the Cumberlands: A Biography of a Depressed Area*, his searing indictment of eastern Kentucky's mining industry. Born in Whitesburg, Letcher County, in 1922, Caudill's roots in eastern Kentucky ran deep. His grandfather's grandfather, James Caudill, was one of the first white settlers in what would become Letcher County, in 1792. Harry Caudill served as an infantryman in Italy during the Second World War and was awarded a Purple Heart for wounds received in combat. His left foot was so badly mangled by shell fragments that he walked with a limp for the rest of his life. After the war he attended law school at the University of Kentucky, then returned to Whitesburg and opened a one-man law practice. Most of his clients were poor, and he came to know their problems well. He also served three two-year terms as a Democratic state representative between 1954 and 1962, an experience he found dispiriting. He sponsored a bill to limit strip mining, but by the time it became a law it had been larded with so many loopholes that he declared it "damn near worthless." He did not hold his fellow lawmakers in high esteem. "Of all American politicians," he later wrote, "the small-bore officials who run the states are the most greedy and least scrupulous." He didn't care much for the electorate either. In an essay he wrote for *Harper's* magazine in 1960, he said he was elected to the legislature only after "paying off citizens of my district with the money and whiskey they demanded in return for their votes." The essay was published anonymously.

Given to verbal grandiloquence ("What an inspired surprise!" he'd thunder when he answered the phone. "To what do I owe the signal honor of this communication?"), Caudill was a gifted writer. He said he decided to write *Night* in the spring of 1960, when he was asked to speak at an eighth-grade graduation ceremony at a coal camp school.

> The seven graduates received their diplomas in the dilapidated two-room building which had sheltered two generations of their forbears. One of the graduates had been orphaned by a mining accident, and the father of another wheezed and gasped with silicosis. The fathers of three others were jobless. The little ceremony was opened with the singing of "America the Beautiful," our most stirring patriotic hymn. The irony of the words, sung so lustily in such a setting, inspired the writing of this book.

He dictated the manuscript to his wife, Anne, and sent it to his friends Mary and Barry Bingham Sr., the publishers of the *Louisville Courier-Journal*, who sent it to their son-in-law, A. Whitney Ellsworth, who was an editor for the *Atlantic* in New York. Ellsworth (who went on to become the first publisher of the *New York Review of Books*) forwarded the manuscript to the publisher Little, Brown, which paid Caudill a $1,000 advance for the book.

Night Comes to the Cumberlands was officially released on July 9, 1963. In 394 pages bristling with anger and contempt, Caudill methodically indicted the timber and coal companies that devastated the landscape with clear-cuts and strip mines, and the corrupt state and local officials who did nothing to stop them. Caudill was not opposed to coal mining per se—he even owned an interest in a small mining company—but he deplored strip mining, which he called "a terrible new emasculation of [the Cumberland plateau's] physical resources." Exploitation is a running theme in *Night*. "Coal has always cursed the land in which it lies," Caudill wrote.

> When men begin to wrest it from the earth it leaves a legacy of foul streams, hideous slag heaps and polluted air. It peoples this transformed land with blind and crippled men and with widows and orphans. It is an extractive industry which takes all away and restores nothing. It mars but never beautifies. It corrupts but never purifies.

Caudill did not spare his neighbors in his critique. He criticized the mountaineers' "tenacious anti-intellectualism," their exceptionally high birth rates, and their growing dependence on "welfarism." He bemoaned the "sustained flight of humanity" from the mountains: "As the more intelligent and ambitious people moved out of the plateau the percentage of mental defectives relative to the total population rose sharply."

In recent years, *Night* has been criticized as anecdotal rather than rigorously academic. Caudill could be a sloppy researcher. He was given to quoting anonymous sources, and, like most raconteurs, he was prone to exaggeration. The historian David McCullough interviewed Caudill for a lengthy profile in *American Heritage* magazine in 1969. Afterward, an incredulous McCullough asked a mutual friend, Loyal Jones, whether everything Caudill had told him was true.

"Well," Jones explained to McCullough, "there are two kinds of truth."

Jones laughs as he tells me about the episode. It is a mild November day in 2018. We are chatting in his room at an assisted-living facility in Richmond, Kentucky. His cat, a small orange tabby named Honey, keeps rubbing against my legs to get my attention. Born in 1928, Jones was one of eight children of tenant farmers in Appalachian North Carolina who raised chickens and hogs and grew vegetables. "We had plenty to eat," Loyal says. "I hardly noticed the Great Depression." As the executive director of the Council of the Southern Mountains, an influential nonprofit agency, and later as the founder and director of the Appalachian Studies program at Berea College, Jones was at the center of the many dramas that played out as the War on Poverty unfolded across Appalachia, and he knew Harry Caudill well. "Harry was a colorful writer and a great talker," he tells me. "He was a teller of tales, in the Appalachian tradition of tall tales. I liked Harry and loved his stories. Nobody could've written *Night Comes to the Cumberlands* but Harry Caudill. It has defects, but it was the most important book about Appalachia in that era."

Some of the writing in *Night* seems hopelessly dated today—a passing reference to "the imported Mexican 'wetback'" is especially jarring—but Caudill was impressively prescient in places. He decried the infatuation with sports at the expense of academics: "Rare is the high school whose football coach is not paid far more than its chemistry, mathematics and English teachers." He anticipated the opioid scourge by four decades, noting the "families here and there . . . enthralled to narcotics." And he lamented the fact that the federal government spent more on foreign aid than on development programs in Appalachia: "Men whose revolutionary forbears died for the slogan 'Death to tyrants!' have voted vast slush funds for Saudi Arabia, an absolute monarchy and one of the few lands where human chattel slavery is still legal."*

It hardly needs to be said that the book won Caudill few fans among his neighbors. As one reviewer noted, "What he has to say in *Night Comes to the Cumberlands* will not get him elected as the first citizen of Letcher County, or any other county in Eastern Kentucky." Privately, Caudill worried some harm might come to him or his family as a result of the book.

Outside the mountains, however, the reviews were glowing. "With devastating candor and clarity, dismay and disgust, humor and hope, Harry Caudill has taken a long look at the Cumberland plateau," the Appalachian writer Wilma Dykeman wrote in the *Chicago Tribune*.

---

* Although Saudi Arabia officially abolished slavery in 1962, the practice continued to be widespread into the 1970s.

"One hopes *Night Comes to the Cumberlands* will be widely read," wrote the Kentucky novelist Harriette Simpson Arnow in her review in the *New York Times*. The book came to the attention of President John F. Kennedy, who urged his aides to read it.

Sales were middling—the book made Caudill famous but not rich— yet *Night Comes to the Cumberlands* would take a place alongside Rachel Carson's *Silent Spring* as one of the most consequential books of the second half of the twentieth century. In 2013, on the fiftieth anniversary of its publication, the *Lexington Herald-Leader* called *Night* "a book that forever changed Appalachia."

In October 1963, three months after *Night* was published, the veteran *New York Times* correspondent Homer Bigart, who'd won two Pulitzer Prizes covering the Second World War and the Korean War, went to eastern Kentucky to see for himself whether things were as bad as Harry Caudill claimed.

They were.

Bigart's story ran on the front page of the Sunday *Times* on October 20, 1963.

"In the Cumberland Mountains of eastern Kentucky," it began, "tens of thousands of unemployed coal miners and subsistence farmers face another winter of idleness and grinding poverty." Their jobs replaced by machines, the miners could find no work and subsisted on government handouts. "So the mountains have become a vast ghetto of unemployables," Bigart wrote. "Crowds of listless, defeated men hang around the county courthouses of the region." Bigart told of unemployed miners who feigned blindness to collect disability checks or abandoned their wives and children to make them eligible for relief. He saw mountainsides "slashed with ugly terraces, where bulldozers and steam shovels have stripped away the forest to get at the coal beneath," and creek beds "littered with garbage, choked with boulders and silt dislodged by strip-mine operations." One schoolhouse that he visited "looked like an abandoned farm shed."

> The interior of the school was unfit for cattle. Daylight shone through gaping holes between rotted planks; most of the tarpaper on the outside was missing. There was a hole in the roof where the stovepipe should have been.

> Mrs. Stone [the teacher, Ruth Stone] said she could not light a fire because the pipe was missing. The stove was so badly cracked she was afraid to use it. Fortunately the days had been warm but cold weather was imminent.

Everywhere Bigart went he encountered malnourished children. "I've seen children who are pot-bellied and anemic," Randall D. Collins, the physician in charge of Letcher County's public health programs, told Bigart. "I've seen children eat dirt out of chimneys. Of 8,200 children in Letcher County, 75 to 85 percent are underweight." The federal government's new school lunch program offered no relief from hunger in schools without electricity or running water. The public health officer for Knott and Leslie Counties estimated that 75 percent of the children in those counties had intestinal parasites such as hookworm. Children throughout the region suffered from vitamin deficiencies.

President Kennedy read Bigart's exposé and was said to be "shocked." He felt it was "an intolerable situation for a nation rich enough to spend billions on foreign aid," the *New York Times* reported. Kennedy ordered his aides to propose an emergency relief package for eastern Kentucky before the winter set in. A $45 million aid package was sent to Congress in early November. (It would not pass because conservatives objected to the cost.)

Meanwhile, JFK announced plans to visit eastern Kentucky to personally assess the situation there. The trip was scheduled for the following month: December 1963. At his last cabinet meeting before leaving for Dallas, Kennedy was doodling on a notepad. Over and over he wrote a single word: "poverty."

2

Dysgenics

HARRY CAUDILL NOT ONLY CATALOGED Appalachia's many problems; he also proposed a solution: the creation of a Southern Mountain Authority— something akin to the Tennessee Valley Authority, the government-owned corporation created by Congress in 1933 to improve the lives of people living in Tennessee and portions of five bordering states. (Ironically, it was the TVA's insatiable hunger for coal to fuel its power plants that contributed to eastern Kentucky's degradation.) Widely considered the most successful New Deal program, the TVA oversaw numerous public works projects—rural electrification, flood control, reforestation, agricultural and industrial development—that vastly improved living standards throughout the Tennessee Valley.

Caudill believed a Southern Mountain Authority—a TVA for Appalachia—was the only solution to the region's problems. "The experience of the T.V.A. indicates that a Southern Mountain Authority created and financed by Congress for the purpose of bringing the region of the Southern mountains abreast of the nation generally could accomplish the greater part of its mission in two or three decades," Caudill wrote in 1963.

Of course, a Southern Mountain Authority was never created, although Congress did establish the Appalachian Regional Commission in 1965. While the ARC has accomplished much—by one estimate, the programs it funded reduced poverty in the region by 7.6 percent between 1960 and 2000—eastern Kentucky still lags well behind the national averages in income, life expectancy, and education.

Caudill came to consider the ARC a failure, and as he grew older, he was gripped by the same hopelessness and despair he had so ably chronicled in *Night Comes to the Cumberlands.* "The poverty that is associated with our region is accompanied by passivity and dependence and I see no hope for allaying it," Caudill wrote in an August 1974 letter to the Nobel Prize–winning physicist turned amateur geneticist William Shockley. "I have come full circle in my thinking and have reluctantly concluded that the poverty that called into being the Appalachian Regional Commission is largely genetic in origin and is largely irreducible." Caudill had come to embrace Shockley's theory of "dysgenics," the belief that less intelligent people procreate faster than smarter people, resulting in a gradual dumbing down of the gene pool and, ultimately, the decline and fall of civilization. Shockley, a paranoid eccentric who shared the 1956 Nobel Prize in Physics for inventing the transistor but had no formal training in genetics, also believed white people were intellectually superior to black people, based on the results of IQ tests created and administered by white people. It was kooky, racist stuff, but Harry Caudill bought it, groping, perhaps, for a way to explain eastern Kentucky's woes. "In conclusion I will say that I know absolutely nothing about the issue of white vs. black intelligence," Caudill wrote Shockley.

> We have few blacks in this area and practically all my observations have dealt with whites. There is no doubt in my mind at the present time that our welfare programs and general humanitarian principles and practices have contrived to effectively repeal the first law of nature so that young and old alike survive to procreate. The dull, dependent and welfare-supported are outbreeding the intelligent and the ambitious. This has, in my opinion, planted a deadly genetic time bomb in our society.

Caudill and Shockley would meet later that year in Whitesburg to plan the implementation of a program of paid, voluntary sterilization in the mountains. Unsurprisingly, funding was nowhere to be found and nothing ever came of it. Shockley died of prostate cancer in 1989. He was seventy-nine. Harry Caudill, diagnosed with Parkinson's disease, shot himself in the head while sitting underneath a hemlock tree in his yard a year later. He was sixty-eight.

3

Replace Their Despair

ON THE EVENING OF WEDNESDAY, January 8, 1964, just forty-seven days after the murder of John F. Kennedy, Lyndon Johnson delivered his first State of the Union address to a joint session of Congress. Standing at the lectern in the well of the House of Representatives, with House Speaker John McCormack and Senator Carl Hayden, president pro tem of the Senate, seated behind him,* Johnson outlined a progressive agenda that included more funding for schools, roads, and hospitals. The centerpiece, however, was what Johnson described as a "war on poverty."

> Unfortunately, many Americans live on the outskirts of hope—some because of their poverty, and some because of their color, and all too many because of both. Our task is to help replace their despair with opportunity.

---

* Hayden occupied the seat usually occupied by the vice president, who also serves as the president of the Senate. At the time, however, the vice presidency was vacant. There was no mechanism for appointing a new vice president after Johnson ascended to the presidency upon Kennedy's death. The vice presidency would remain vacant until January 1965, when Hubert Humphrey assumed the office following his election as Johnson's running mate. Had Johnson died in the interim, Speaker John McCormack would have become president. The Twenty-Fifth Amendment, which took effect in 1967, now allows a president to appoint a vice president in the event the office becomes vacant. (The appointee must be confirmed by a majority vote of both houses of Congress.)

This administration today, here and now, declares uncondi-
tional war on poverty in America. I urge this Congress and all
Americans to join with me in that effort.

It will not be a short or easy struggle, no single weapon or
strategy will suffice, but we shall not rest until that war is won.
The richest Nation on earth can afford to win it. We cannot
afford to lose it. One thousand dollars invested in salvaging an
unemployable youth today can return $40,000 or more in his
lifetime.

Saying one-fifth of all American families lacked the resources to
meet their basic needs, Johnson proposed a joint "federal-local effort"
to "pursue poverty . . . wherever it exists—in city slums and small towns,
in sharecropper shacks or in migrant worker camps, on Indian Reserva-
tions, among whites as well as Negroes, among the young as well as the
aged, in the boom towns and in the depressed areas."

Johnson also promised to "launch a special effort in the chronically
distressed areas of Appalachia."

The "chief weapons" in this war, Johnson said, would be "better
schools, and better health, and better homes, and better training, and
better job opportunities to help more Americans, especially young
Americans, escape from squalor and misery and unemployment rolls
where other citizens help to carry them." He proposed a dizzying array
of programs: area redevelopment programs, job programs, public works
programs, food programs, education programs, a domestic version of
the Peace Corps, unemployment insurance, health insurance for the
elderly, new minimum wage laws, more libraries, more schools, more
hospitals, more nursing homes, nurse-training programs, housing and
urban renewal programs, mass transit programs, work study and student
loan programs—all of which, he insisted, would benefit all Americans,
not just those in poverty.

Every American will benefit by the extension of social security
to cover the hospital costs of their aged parents. Every American
community will benefit from the construction or moderniza-
tion of schools, libraries, hospitals, and nursing homes, from

the training of more nurses and from the improvement of urban renewal in public transit.

At forty-one minutes, it was the shortest State of the Union address in thirty years—and one of the most ambitious ever. The *New York Times* called it "a strong and compassionate statement of the things Congress should and must do to build a better America." Republicans were less impressed. Barry Goldwater said Johnson had "out-Roosevelted Roosevelt, out-Kennedyed Kennedy, and even made Truman look like some kind of piker."

"I can't think of a part of the United States or any people he hasn't promised something to," said Goldwater in New Hampshire, where he was campaigning for the Republican presidential nomination. "There is not one single field in which he is not trying to move in and take over your lives."

Republicans called the bill a "hodgepodge" and an election year stunt, and they howled at the cost of it all (an estimated $1 billion a year for the next five years), but the Democrats controlled both chambers of Congress and Johnson was a persuasive lobbyist. On August 20, 1964, less than eight months after proposing the bevy of programs that collectively have come to be known as the War on Poverty, Johnson signed the Economic Opportunity Act in a ceremony outside the White House, on the steps overlooking the Rose Garden. "Today, for the first time in the history of the human race, a great nation is willing to make, and able to make, a commitment to eliminate poverty among our people," LBJ said that day. "I firmly believe that as of this moment a new opportunity is dawning and a new era of progress is opening for us all."

Although the War on Poverty was in some ways a continuation of President Kennedy's policies, Johnson's support for it was heartfelt. He'd grown up poor in central Texas, and as a young man he'd taught at a school for Mexican American children. "I shall never forget the faces of the boys and the girls in that little Welhausen Mexican School," he recalled when he was president, "and I remember even yet the pain of realizing and knowing then that college was closed to practically every one of those children because they were too poor."

The signing of the Economic Opportunity Act gave great hope to many living in impoverished areas, including eastern Kentucky. "The anti-poverty legislation just signed by President Johnson means to some in this depressed area a crack in the wall of despair," Associated Press reporter Jak Martin wrote from Hazard.

The new law established a federal agency, the Office of Economic Opportunity, or OEO, to oversee the smorgasbord of antipoverty programs it created. Robert Kennedy, still the attorney general, was thought to be the perfect choice to head the OEO. But, as the historian Edward R. Schmitt wrote, "The new president saw the poverty program as his chance to become the Franklin Roosevelt of the second half of the twentieth century, [and] Robert Kennedy's interest posed a threat to exclusive popular identification of Johnson as poverty warrior in chief." Instead, Johnson tapped RFK's brother-in-law Sargent Shriver to lead the OEO. Shriver, who was married to John and Robert's sister Eunice, was already the director of the Peace Corps, but Johnson cajoled him into taking on the second job. Appointing Shriver to oversee the OEO was, Schmitt wrote, a "political masterstroke. [Johnson] thereby inoculated himself against charges that he was moving away from the intentions of John Kennedy while making the initiative his own."

In any event, Robert Kennedy had other plans. On August 25, 1964, just five days after Johnson signed the Economic Opportunity Act, Kennedy announced that he was running for the US Senate—from New York. (Running in Massachusetts was not an option: the incumbent running for reelection in 1964 was his brother Ted.) He made the announcement at Gracie Mansion, the official residence of New York's mayors, with his wife, Ethel, at his side. "There may be some who believe where a candidate voted in the past is more important than his capacity to serve the state," he said. "I cannot in fairness ask them to vote for me." But he then went on to list his attachments to the Empire State: "I attended New York schools for six years before my father became Ambassador to Great Britain, and I have once again established residence in this state." (According to RFK biographer Larry Tye, "He leased from a wealthy designer a twenty-five-room Dutch Colonial house in Glen Cove on Long Island, staging his family there for press events but seldom staying himself.")

Immediately after making his announcement, Kennedy flew to Atlantic City, where the Democratic National Convention was underway at Convention Hall. On the convention's final night, Kennedy introduced a short film about his murdered brother. As he mounted the dais and approached the podium, he was met with thunderous, rapturous applause, an ovation that overwhelmed the hall and lasted anywhere from eleven to seventeen minutes (accounts vary). "Through it all," the *Baltimore Sun* noted, "the 38-year-old Attorney General, who will resign soon to become a Democratic senatorial candidate in New York, stood quietly and sadly, without waving, without smiling."

4

Tom Fletcher

On the morning of Friday, April 24, 1964, Tom Fletcher, an unemployed thirty-eight-year-old millworker and miner who lived with his wife and their eight children in a small house just outside the Martin County town of Inez, Kentucky, was surprised when two Secret Service agents showed up at his house unannounced and told him the president of the United States wanted to stop by to say hello later that day. Fletcher told the agents that would be fine.

A few hours later, Lyndon Johnson swooped down on Inez in his presidential helicopter, making good on his predecessor's promise to visit eastern Kentucky. But the trip was less a fact-finding mission than a publicity stunt; at the time, the Economic Opportunity Act was still pending before Congress.

Wearing a dark suit, the president took a seat on a pile of wood on Fletcher's front porch. The two men chatted quietly for about thirty minutes. Johnson was uncharacteristically subdued. Fletcher told the president that he'd earned only about $400 the previous year, mostly by scavenging coal from abandoned mines. He'd dropped out of school after the fourth grade, as had his two oldest children, an eighteen-year-old son and a seventeen-year-old daughter.

The short visit made a deep impression on Johnson, who later wrote, "My determination was reinforced that day to use the powers of the presidency to the fullest extent that I could, to persuade America to help all its Tom Fletchers."

President Johnson on Tom Fletcher's front porch in Inez, Kentucky, on April 24, 1964. *Cecil Stoughton; LBJ Presidential Library*

In newspaper reports the day after the president's visit, Fletcher's humble home was variously described as "dilapidated," "rickety," "a tar-paper shack," or "a ramshackle cabin," descriptions that rankled Fletcher, his family later recalled, because he thought the house was "in fairly decent shape."

The visit made Fletcher a reluctant bellwether for poverty in Appalachia. On milestone anniversaries of Johnson's visit, reporters and camera crews would make the trek to Inez to see how the Fletchers were doing. The answer was always the same: not well. Immediately after Johnson's visit, Fletcher was given a job on a road crew as part of a federal jobs program for unemployed fathers (widely called the Happy Pappy program). When that job ended, he enrolled in a job-training program to learn how to be a mechanic but never found a job. In 1969 he broke his leg and never again worked regularly. Fletcher's wife died of breast cancer.

In 1986, when he was sixty, Fletcher married Mary Porter, who was forty years his junior. Fletcher and his second wife had two children. Their daughter, three-year-old Ella, died suddenly in January 1992.

Doctors believed it was the result of an epileptic seizure. A month later their four-year-old son, Tommy Jr., was hospitalized. Doctors found he had suffered an overdose of the painkiller Darvon. The boy survived, but investigators exhumed Ella's body and found she had been poisoned as well. Tom and Mary were arrested and charged with Ella's murder. WAR ON POVERTY SYMBOL ACCUSED OF MURDER, read the unfortunate headline in the *New York Times*. Mary eventually confessed and exonerated Tom. She said she'd poisoned the children because she wanted to collect $5,000 in burial insurance. Mary was sentenced to twenty-five years in prison. She was released in 2017.

When a reporter interviewed Tom Fletcher in 1994, on the thirtieth anniversary of Johnson's visit, he was still living in the same humble house that the president had visited. His only income was $284 in monthly disability payments. And he was fed up with reporters asking him if he was still poor. "I'm getting tired of it," he said. "After all this time, I'd think they would be letting it go."

The War on Poverty had lifted millions of Americans out of poverty, but not Tom Fletcher. He died in 2004. He was seventy-eight.

5

An Article in *Life*

THE ARTICLE THAT APPEARED IN *Life* magazine in January 1968 put eastern Kentucky in the national spotlight once again. Written by David Nevin, a veteran *Life* reporter whose usual beat was the civil rights movement, and illustrated with photographs by a noted photojournalist named Bob Gomel, the thirty-five-hundred-word spread profiled mountain families whose land was being destroyed by strip mines—and the families couldn't do anything about it. The mineral rights had been sold decades earlier, often at the beginning of the century—long before large-scale strip mining was technologically feasible—and often for as little as fifty cents an acre. These agreements, known as broad-form deeds, gave mining companies the right to do practically anything to mine the coal beneath the surface of their land. The companies didn't need to obtain the landowner's permission, nor were they required to pay compensation for damages. Only "wanton, arbitrary or malicious" conduct was prohibited—a high bar indeed.

In the late nineteenth century, when it became apparent that the central Appalachian Mountains held untold millions of tons of coal, the corporations that required the mineral to fire their furnaces—most notably United States Steel and Bethlehem Steel—and their various subsidiaries sent waves of agents into the hills to buy the rights to extract the coal that had been buried beneath mountains, unexploited for eons. These rich seams of black carbon would fuel, literally, the American economy for more than a century. The agents were not uniformly ethical. It was not necessary to purchase land outright, only the rights to extract the minerals the land held. Their device—the broad-form deed—exploited a relatively new concept in land ownership: horizontal severance.

In common law, a landowner held title to his property from the center of the earth to the "heavens above." Beginning in the sixteenth century, however, the concept of horizontal severance emerged in England. The Crown required huge quantities of saltpeter—potassium nitrate, a surprisingly versatile mineral that can be used as a fertilizer, to make gunpowder, and to preserve food. Accordingly, the monarch's agents were authorized to enter upon private property and extract the mineral from the earth. The landowner retained all rights to the property above the ground, the Crown all rights below. This separated the land into multiple strata that could be owned or controlled by multiple owners. (More recently this concept has been expanded to include the "air rights" above a property. After New York's Penn Station was demolished in 1963, the Pennsylvania Railroad leased the air rights above ground level to the developers of Madison Square Garden.)

When landowners in eastern Kentucky began selling their mineral rights, mining was almost entirely an underground activity. A shaft would be bored into the side of a mountain. Men with pickaxes and shovels would be sent in to mine the coal. A small building might be erected at the entrance to the mineshaft and a short section of train tracks laid to the nearest main line. But most landowners were unfazed by these alterations to their property. For the most part, underground mining was minimally disruptive and practically invisible. Strip mining was neither.

The broad-form deed would haunt generations of mountain families, many of whom believed they had been swindled out of the rights to valuable minerals on their property. Many who signed the deeds— often with a shaky X—were illiterate and undereducated and did not fully comprehend the implications of the agreements. "The meek shall inherit the earth," goes an old saying in Appalachia, "but not the mineral rights."

In 1956 Kentucky's highest court ruled that the broad-form deed applied to strip mining even though that method of mineral extraction was unknown when most of the deeds were executed. The court also ruled that mining companies were not liable for any damage to the property that resulted from strip mining. "The owner of the mineral has the paramount right to the use of the surface in the prosecution of its business for any purpose of necessity or convenience," the court ruled in *Buchanan v. Watson*. The decision also stated, "The rule has become so firmly established that it is a rule of property law governing the rights under many mineral deeds covering much acreage in Eastern Kentucky. To disturb this rule now would create great confusion and much hardship in a segment of an industry that can ill-afford such a blow." The state's high court would reaffirm the ruling in June 1968 (*Martin v. Kentucky Oak Mining Co.*).*

For *Life*, David Nevin focused on two families at war with strip mine operators. Fifty-seven-year-old Cecil Combs, his wife, and her three grown sons from a previous marriage lived on a "vertical farm," thirty acres on a steep hillside along Pigeon Roost Creek in Jackson County. Debris from a strip mine at the top of the hill—uprooted trees, boulders, and tons of rocks and dirt—was raining down on their property. But Combs was powerless to stop the assault. His family had sold the mineral rights decades earlier, so his only solution was to build an earthen dam around his house to block the debris—and hope it would hold.

The other family profiled was an elderly couple, Tom and Rebecca Fuson, and their four grown sons. The Fusons owned 180 acres of land near Pineville but lost the property in a title dispute with a mining company. The family refused to surrender the land without a fight, and when the mining equipment came one day, there was gunfire. The sheriff was called out to investigate, and more gunfire ensued. Old Tom Fuson, eighty-one, was shot dead through the chest.

The characters in Nevin's story were straight out of central casting—Combs was described as toothless, illiterate, permanently disabled in a bar fight; the Fusons, Nevin wrote, "hunted and made whisky and

---

* In 1988 the Kentucky legislature finally amended the state constitution to clarify that broad-form deeds could only allow extraction by means that were common when the deeds were executed. Five years later the Supreme Court of Kentucky upheld the amendment. But the damage had been done. Countless landscapes had been ravaged, rivers and streams ruined, homes destroyed.

raised corn and there was a strangely remote quality about the whole family, as if they lived in a world that was slightly different from that of other people"—but their anguish was genuine. Resistance to strip mining in eastern Kentucky had been building slowly since late November 1965, when a sixty-one-year-old widow named Ollie Combs (no relation to Cecil Combs) galvanized opposition to the practice. The Widow Combs, as she was inevitably referred to, sat in front of a bulldozer that had come to begin stripping her mountainside property in Honey Gap Hollow, Knott County. Combs and two of her sons were arrested for violating an injunction against such protests. A Kentucky state trooper and Knott County sheriff Oliver "Bud" Hylton carried Combs away by her arms and legs. "About halfway down the hill, I began to get kind of heavy," Combs later recalled in an oral history interview for Alice Lloyd College. "One of the police officers said, 'Mrs. Combs, if you'll get up and walk, I'll buy you a cup of coffee.' I said, 'I don't drink coffee.'" Combs and her sons were subsequently sentenced to twenty hours in jail. They were released on the morning of Thanksgiving Day.

A photograph of Combs being carried away from her home was published in newspapers nationwide and became a defining image of the anti–strip mining movement. Sheriff Hylton had ordered the photographer, Bill Strode of the *Louisville Courier-Journal*, to stop taking pictures of the arrest. When Strode refused, he was also arrested, for trespassing. Hylton tried to seize Strode's camera, but when the two men tussled over it, the strap around Strode's neck broke and the camera tumbled down the mountain. Hylton was unaware that Strode had already stashed the film down the front of his pants. In 1967 the *Courier-Journal* was awarded a Pulitzer Prize for its coverage of strip mining.

The publicity surrounding the arrest of the Widow Combs shamed the mining company into abandoning its plans to strip the property. "It's where I raised my family and it's the only home I ever really owned," Ollie Combs later said. "I told them, 'Go under the hill; you can go under the hill and get coal—people used to get it that way—go under the hill and get the coal.'"

Ollie Combs was a courageous woman. Few residents of eastern Kentucky were willing to take on the coal companies and their allies in local politics and law enforcement. "Most of the mountain people feel powerless and beaten," David Nevin wrote in *Life*. "This country is in the heart of the Appalachian rural poverty belt. The people are a welfare generation of out-of-work coal miners. Their shacks are weathered and sagging, and the creeks are filled with rubbish and offal."

It was the Second World War that made strip mining possible. Technology developed during the war made practical the huge machines required to move earth: augers, shovels, and bulldozers. By 1968 twenty-story-tall "super shovels" could chomp off 175 tons of earth—what the mining industry calls "overburden"—in a single bite, exposing seams of coal for smaller shovels to recover. Today, 14,000-ton bucket-wheel excavators can move more than 500,000 tons of overburden in a day.

Strip mining was cheaper, safer, and more efficient than underground mining, and it required fewer workers. Environmentally, however, it was a disaster.

Debris from strip mines slid down hillsides, contaminating creeks with heavy metals and sulfuric acid. Mining companies were not required to restore the land they stripped, leaving it vulnerable to erosion. Without ground cover to absorb rainfall, hollows flooded. Ecosystems were laid to waste. Wildlife habitats were obliterated, flora simply wiped out.

In the *Life* article, Harry Caudill, described as an "eloquent mountain lawyer," was quoted at length. "When man destroys his land, he begins to destroy himself," Caudill said. "This land may not recover fully for a century."

On January 20, 1968, shortly after that issue of *Life* hit newsstands, Caudill dictated to his wife a letter to be sent to Robert Kennedy. The date, coincidentally, was exactly one year before the next presidential inauguration.

Dear Senator Kennedy,

Perhaps you have seen the article in the January 12, 1968 issue of LIFE magazine on the destruction of eastern Kentucky's land and people by surface miners. It was written by David Nevin, a LIFE editor, and if you have not had an opportunity to look at it I hope you will do so.

People here in the mountains look to you as something of a national Senator, a Senator for all parts of America alike, and for that reason I hope you will be able to find time in your busy life to take an interest in their problems.

To date the WAR on POVERTY has been little more than a hollow pretense here and the forces that impoverish eastern Kentucky continue to run rampant. Unless changes are made soon, nothing will have been accomplished with the exception of the spending of substantial sums of money with disappointment to many people whose hopes have been unduly raised.

Please permit me to invite you to come to eastern Kentucky for a visit. My wife, Anne, and I would like to have an opportunity to show you some of our terribly urgent land and people problems and there are other groups and many individuals within the area who would be delighted to have you here and to talk to you. . . .

Very sincerely yours,

Harry M. Caudill

It's not clear whether Kennedy had ever met Caudill, but he certainly knew who he was. After he read the letter, Kennedy scribbled in the upper right-hand corner: "Good fellow—author of Night Comes to the Cumberlands."

6

Poverty Obsessed

ROBERT KENNEDY'S INTEREST IN POVERTY was practically pathological, and it has preoccupied and perplexed his biographers for decades. His own circumstances were anything but impecunious, of course. His father, Joseph P. Kennedy Sr., was a millionaire many times over; in 1957 *Fortune* magazine estimated his worth to be $250 million (more than $2 billion in today's dollars). He accumulated wealth through many channels: stocks, real estate, liquor, motion pictures, banking. His wife, Rose, whom he married in 1914, was the daughter of John "Honey Fitz" Fitzgerald, who served two terms as mayor of Boston between 1906 and 1914.

Robert Francis Kennedy was born November 20, 1925, the seventh of Joseph and Rose Kennedy's nine children. He attended a series of private schools. Summers were spent in Hyannis Port, the winter holidays in Palm Beach. He was a sensitive boy and prone to melancholia. His older brother Jack nicknamed him Black Robert.

He served in the navy from 1944 to 1946 but saw no combat during the Second World War. His service included a short stint aboard the USS *Joseph P. Kennedy Jr.*, a destroyer named for his eldest brother, who was killed when his plane exploded on a mission en route from England in 1944.*

---

* Kennedy's plane was loaded with Torpex, an explosive 50 percent more powerful than TNT. The plan was for the crew to aim the plane at its target (U-boat pens in the North

It was a trip to Egypt in 1948 that first opened Robert Kennedy's eyes to crushing poverty. He was twenty-two and fresh out of Harvard. His father arranged for him to travel to the Middle East as a sort of roving correspondent for the *Boston Post*. "No middle class at all," he wrote in his journal in Cairo. "The lower class are absolute peons. . . . Poor children have a terrible existence with flies crawling in eyes & nose & it seems to bother them not one iota. They know no better." Kennedy never imagined such poverty existed in the United States—until his brother ran for president in 1960.

Winning West Virginia's Democratic primary was critical to Jack's candidacy.* As Jack's campaign manager, Bobby crisscrossed the state, stumping for his brother. This brought him into close contact with Appalachian poverty for the first time—"hungry, hollow-eyed children, dispirited families living on cornmeal and surplus lard, gray, dismal towns, despair about the future," as the Kennedy family confidant and historian Arthur M. Schlesinger described it—and, like his brother, Robert was appalled. He scarcely believed such poverty could exist in the richest nation on earth. He wanted to learn more about the problem.

As US attorney general and, later, senator from New York, he walked the ghettos of Washington and New York. In April 1967 he toured the Mississippi Delta, where he found poor black residents living in conditions that left him shaken: listless children with bellies distended by hunger, families in shotgun shacks with no running water, homes with no furniture or utensils. In Cleveland, Mississippi, a local official estimated that 95 percent of the town's children were malnourished. "I've been to third-world countries and I've never seen anything like this," Kennedy told his aide Peter Edelman.

Biographer Larry Tye wrote that the Mississippi trip is "often cited as Bobby's epiphany regarding the depth of poverty in America." By 1968 Kennedy was obsessed with poverty. He had become, in Schlesinger's

---

Sea), put it on autopilot, and bail out. But the plane exploded shortly after taking off, with no chance for the crew to evacuate. The mission was widely considered suicidal. Kennedy volunteered for it even though he had completed his allotment of combat missions.

* At one campaign stop in West Virginia, an old coal miner asked John Kennedy if it was true that he had never worked a day in his life. "I guess there is some truth to that," Kennedy answered. "Well," the miner said, "you haven't missed a goddamn thing."

words, the "Tribune of the Underclass." "Kennedy dwells on the tragedy of the poor," the *Washington Post*'s Richard Harwood noted during Kennedy's brief 1968 presidential campaign. Kennedy was a "'one-issue' candidate," Harwood noted, and that issue was poverty.

How did Robert F. Kennedy, born into enormous wealth, come to be a champion of the poor? Perhaps it was a genuine expression of his deep religious conviction, a manifestation of his Catholic faith and Christ's admonition to love your neighbor as yourself. Perhaps it was simply a cold political calculation. Perhaps it was the result of his brother's assassination. The journalist Nicholas Lemann believed Kennedy "became convinced that poverty-fighting had been at the core of his brother's work, work that he now had to carry forward." More likely it was a mixture of all these. Undoubtedly the issue aroused his preternatural sense of empathy. A friend of Kennedy's once said, "I think Bobby knows precisely what it feels like to be a very old woman."

In his book *President of the Other America: Robert Kennedy and the Politics of Poverty*, Edward R. Schmitt contended that Kennedy was "guided by a distinctive communitarian conception of government."

> Kennedy's search for community was central to most—though not all—of the domestic issues he engaged. His application of the notion of community was elastic, at times fuzzy, and often perhaps naive. Kennedy would be drawn to the issue of poverty as a threat to all levels of community in the United States, and his policy proposals would reflect a consistent vision of the interrelationship between the individual, the local "grassroots" community, and the national community.

Harry Caudill's invitation to visit Kentucky landed on Kennedy's desk at a propitious moment. Kennedy wanted to show that poverty wasn't just a black problem; he wanted to shine a light on white poverty too. "It's obviously a problem that crosses racial lines," says Kennedy aide Peter Edelman, "and [Kennedy believed] the country should know that." Kennedy considered visiting South Carolina, but, according to Edelman, South Carolina senator Fritz Hollings begged Kennedy not to go. Hollings, a Democrat, was up for reelection that year. Edelman recalls, "He said to RFK, 'Please don't come to South Carolina. I promise that I will do the work to expose it [hunger] in my own state.' And Hollings did do that."

So, instead, Kennedy accepted Harry Caudill's invitation. He would go to Kentucky.

7

A Pioneer in Opposition Research

PETER EDELMAN WAS ONLY TWENTY-SIX when he helped Robert Kennedy win a seat in the US Senate in 1964, winning for himself a plum job on Kennedy's staff and a front-row seat to one of the most eventful periods in American history.

Born and raised in Minneapolis, Edelman came from a middle-class Jewish family. His father was a lawyer, a "decent, community-spirited man." His mother, who died of colon cancer when he was fifteen, was "a smart, shy, musical woman who mistrusted country clubs and wealth." He got good grades in high school and went to Harvard. He got good grades at Harvard and went to Harvard Law. He clerked for US Supreme Court justice Arthur Goldberg and seemed headed for a lucrative career in private practice when Goldberg urged him to work for the Kennedy administration instead. "Justice Goldberg told me there would be few administrations like that of President Kennedy in my lifetime and recommended government service," Edelman wrote. He took a job in the Justice Department's civil division, though he rarely came in contact with the attorney general. If they'd bumped into each other in the hallway, Edelman recalled years later, "I doubt that RFK would have put my face together with my name."

When Kennedy ran for the Senate in 1964, however, Edelman's star began to rise. He went to work for the campaign and caught Kennedy's attention by researching the voting record of his opponent, incumbent senator Kenneth Keating, a moderate Republican, and creating a full-page newspaper ad that likened Keating's voting record to Barry Goldwater's. "I had found my niche," Edelman recalled. "I was a pioneer in opposition research." His work caught Kennedy's eye. "Now he knew who I was," Edelman tells me in his office at Georgetown Law School, where he has been on the faculty since 1982. "He was certainly listening to what I was saying."

Shortly after Election Day, Edelman was summoned to the White House for a job interview with the senator-elect. Kennedy had hurt his knee playing touch football and was being examined by the White House doctor, Janet Travell, who had been President Kennedy's personal physician. Edelman watched while Travell *tap-tap-tapped* Kennedy's knee with a reflex hammer in the White House exam room. The knee was fine. Then Edelman and Kennedy went outside, accompanied by Ed Guthman, Kennedy's press secretary. Kennedy leaned against the fender of a car parked on the road between the White House and the Old Executive Office Building and casually asked Edelman, "Are you gonna come work for me?"

"And I'm completely—don't know what to say." Edelman gets a little tongue-tied just recalling the moment. "I thought I was supposed to be grilled. So I said, 'How much would you pay me?' Which was a pretty stupid question. And he said, 'Work that out with Ed,' who was standing there with us. And I said, 'Well, I have this problem: I've been out of law school now for three and a half years and I haven't practiced law.' And he said to me, 'Well, I had that problem and I worked it out.'"

Edelman, whose official title would be legislative assistant, shared his boss's passion for fighting poverty. "You had the civil rights movement at the time," he explains. "Organically, it's perfectly logical that if you're thinking fully about civil rights you have to start thinking that poverty is a major part of that as well. It's an optimistic time, post–World War II expansion, people were feeling that we were on an upward trend in terms of economic capacity, so if you're ever going to have a kind of willingness to reach out and do things differently, the combination of the optimism that went with winning the war and the economic expansion that ensued, that would be a logical time to be more receptive on the question of civil rights and on poverty as well."

Edelman helped plan Kennedy's trip to Mississippi in April 1967. In fact, it was on a scouting trip to Jackson ahead of Kennedy's visit that Edelman met the woman he would marry, Marian Wright, a civil rights lawyer and the first African American woman admitted to the Mississippi Bar. A friend had told him that she would be the best person to show him around the capital. Edelman called her when he arrived, but she said she was too busy preparing a brief to meet with him. He suggested they meet for dinner—"But you've got to eat dinner!" he pleaded—and she acquiesced. "It was a decidedly pleasant evening," Edelman recalled, "even though the conversation was in large part about decidedly unpleasant subjects."

Naturally, Edelman was assigned to arrange Kennedy's trip to Kentucky as well. Like the Mississippi trip, field hearings of the Senate Subcommittee on Employment, Manpower, and Poverty would be held. Kennedy, who sat on the committee, would be joined by Kentucky senator John Sherman Cooper, who also was a member of the committee, as well as Congressman Carl Perkins, who represented eastern Kentucky in the House. Unlike Fritz Hollings, Cooper, a Republican, was not running for reelection in 1968. As for Perkins, a Democrat, his reelection was a foregone conclusion: he'd held the seat for twenty years and would hold it for sixteen more, until his death in 1984. (Senator Cooper would have to drop out of the trip at the last minute after the death of his uncle, leaving Kennedy as the sole committee member on the trip.) Besides assessing antipoverty programs, the trip would serve another purpose: it would give Kennedy a chance to field-test his nascent presidential campaign strategy of appealing to working-class white voters. Officially, Kennedy was still saying he had no plans to run. Unofficially, the campaign's groundwork was already being laid.

Peter Edelman flew to Lexington on February 8 and spent the next four days crisscrossing eastern Kentucky in a rented car, meeting with local politicians, getting briefed on local issues, scouting locations for events, and interviewing potential witnesses for the hearings. He was accompanied by another Kennedy staffer, Tom Johnston, who, as luck would have it, was a Kentucky native, making Edelman's job considerably easier. Edelman met with Harry Caudill, of course, as well as Tom and Pat Gish, the publishers of the *Mountain Eagle*, a daily newspaper in Whitesburg that, unlike most local papers in eastern Kentucky, was unafraid to take on King Coal.

On the morning of Tuesday, February 13, 1968, Senator Robert F. Kennedy flew from Washington to Lexington on Eastern Airlines Flight 659.

Part II

Tuesday,
February 13, 1968

Robert Kennedy conducting a Senate subcommittee hearing in the one-room schoolhouse at
Vortex, Kentucky, on February 13, 1968. The hearing was notably informal. *Michele Farris*

8

1:00 PM—Vortex

AROUND ONE O'CLOCK, the Kennedy motorcade pulled up to a one-room schoolhouse in Vortex, a speck of a town in Wolfe County, about seventy miles southeast of Lexington. By some measures, Wolfe County was the poorest county in the country. It was estimated that five thousand of its sixty-five hundred residents lived below the poverty line.

Determining the poverty line has always been problematic, a political as well as an economic riddle. When LBJ declared the War on Poverty in January 1964, the federal government didn't even have a definition for poverty. It was Mollie Orshansky who came up with one. Born in 1915, Orshansky was the third of six daughters born to Samuel and Fannie Orshansky, Jewish immigrants from Ukraine who settled in the Bronx. Mollie graduated from Hunter College in 1935 with a degree in mathematics and statistics. She wanted to pursue an academic career but found her options limited. In 1939 she went to work for the federal Children's Bureau, researching children's health and nutrition. In 1945 she joined the Department of Agriculture, researching household spending and food consumption. Orshansky was, according to the historian Alice O'Connor, "one of a respected but mostly invisible cadre of women research professionals based at . . . government agencies during the postwar years."

"These women," O'Connor wrote in *Poverty Knowledge*, a history of poverty research, "found job opportunities in federal government and other 'applied' endeavors when university jobs were largely closed off to them, although within government they were often clustered in research bureaus focusing on such traditional 'women's' concerns as social welfare, female labor force participation, families and children, and home economics."

In 1958 Orshansky moved from Agriculture to the Social Security Administration, where she would work until her retirement in 1982. It was there that Orshansky was tasked with estimating the number of American children living in poverty. Using the Department of Agriculture's dietary guidelines, she calculated the minimum income needed to feed a family of four. She determined that approximately a third of the average family's income was spent on food. She calculated the cost of the other essentials—clothes, housing, medical care—and determined that a family of four required a minimum income of $3,165 annually to meet its basic needs. Based on her calculations, Orshansky estimated that between a quarter and a third of all American children were, in her words, "growing up in the gray shadow of poverty."

Orshansky's report, published in the July 1963 issue of the *Social Security Bulletin*, attracted little notice outside government circles at first. But after the War on Poverty was launched the following January, Orshansky's formula for determining the poverty line (officially known as the poverty threshold) became the federal government's de facto definition of poverty—and it has remained so, with remarkably few adjustments, ever since.

In 1977 Orshansky came up with a new formula that would have taken into account falling food prices and rising housing costs. The new formula would have raised the poverty line for a family of four from $5,820 to $6,610 and, in a stroke, increased the official number of people living in poverty from twenty-six million to thirty-six million. That, of course, was politically untenable. Orshansky was resigned to her original formula's fate as a faulty indicator of poverty. "The best that can be said of the measure," she once wrote, "is that at a time when it seemed useful, it was there."

More recent attempts to tweak Orshansky's formula have also been rejected, keeping the poverty rate (and the number of people eligible for benefits) artificially low. Orshansky—who literally defined poverty in the United States—died in 2006. She was ninety-one. In 2017 the poverty line for a family of four was $24,944 and the poverty rate was 12.3 percent.

———————

Inside the dingy schoolhouse in Vortex, Kennedy convened a one-man hearing of the US Senate Subcommittee on Employment, Manpower, and Poverty. An old potbelly stove sat in the center of the room. Bare lightbulbs dangled from the ceiling. On the chalkboard the teacher had written: TUESDAY. WELCOME VISITORS. It was certainly a humble setting for a US Senate committee hearing.

Wearing horn-rimmed glasses and casually standing behind the teacher's large wooden desk with his hands in the pockets of his herringbone jacket, a white handkerchief peeking perfectly out of the breast pocket, Kennedy spoke so softly that the reporters in the back of the room strained to hear him. He began by listing some of the War on Poverty programs, then explained why he'd come to eastern Kentucky.

> What we are going to try to find out in the next two days of hearings is whether the programs have been effective; whether our fellow Americans here in the state of Kentucky and Eastern Kentucky particularly—whether our fellow Americans are receiving enough to eat; whether the programs that have been developed by the government are sufficient and satisfactory. We have a gross national product of $800 billion a year here in the United States. It's not satisfactory and it's not acceptable in our country that any of our citizens do not have enough to eat, and our children do not have enough to eat. . . .
>
> I know this is an area that has suffered in the past. It's unacceptable that the area continues to suffer, and all of us, no matter what area of the country we represent or what states we represent, if there is poverty, and it's your wish to work in various jobs, we must do something about it, and I think the government of the United States can do something about it, I think we can make much more progress than we have in the past; we have the skill, the tools and the desire; we have the energy and

the talent. We must bring to bear the problems that exist, and when we are working with the people of Eastern Kentucky, we are working with some of the most able and courageous people in the United States.

Over the next hour or so, Kennedy heard testimony from five witnesses, who stood or sat across the big desk from him, while newspaper photographers and TV cameramen jostled for position around them. The school's five students—including four siblings—and their teacher, Mrs. Curtis, settled in and watched in rapt attention as a lesson in American civics played out before them in real time.

9

Swango Fugate

SWANGO FUGATE WAS THE FIRST TO TESTIFY. He was an unemployed miner turned community organizer from neighboring Breathitt County. Born in 1908 and named for the doctor who delivered him, Fugate was a father of nine (with four still at home) and a lifelong Republican. He and his wife, Stella, tended a small subsistence farm on their property.

Fugate was the chairman of a group called the Grassroots Citizens Committee of Wolfe and Breathitt Counties. The committee had recently received a $40,000 grant from the Office of Economic Opportunity with few strings attached, only a directive that the money be spent on projects that improve the community. So far the group had spent $1,525 of the grant to build a mile-and-a-quarter-long paved road in a remote hollow about ten miles east of Jackson, the Breathitt County seat. It replaced an old creek-bed road and connected twenty-six families to the countywide road network, markedly improving the quality of their lives.

The Grassroots Citizens Committee planned to use the rest of the money to build two community centers, a grocery co-op, and more paved roads. A subcommittee made up entirely of welfare recipients voted on the projects, which only required the approval of the OEO to implement them. The grant was in line with the OEO's policy of "maximum feasible participation"—giving poor people rather than bureaucrats the power to decide how antipoverty funds should be spent—a policy that nettled local politicians accustomed to controlling federal largesse.

Fugate told the *Louisville Courier-Journal* that one county official had "tried to tell us how to spend the money" but "we didn't pay any attention to him."

"We don't know how we are going to spend what we have left," he told the paper, "but you can bet that a lot of people are going to get roads who never had them before." (Ironically, Fugate never learned to drive.)

"What we are trying to do," Fugate explained to Kennedy, "we are trying to get the poor class of people together, to organize, to help themselves, is our main project."

Kennedy then asked Fugate what he thought of the food stamp program. Fugate replied that food stamps were too expensive.

Contrary to popular belief, food stamps weren't free. It was a policy that dated back to the founding of the program. In October 1933 the Federal Surplus Relief Corporation (FSRC) was established as part of the New Deal. One of the scores of "alphabet agencies" created by Franklin D. Roosevelt to fight the Depression, the FSRC was not nearly as well known as others, such as the Civilian Conservation Corps (CCC), the Federal Deposit Insurance Corporation (FDIC), and the Works Progress Administration (WPA), but its powers were extraordinary.

Ostensibly the FSRC was charged with raising farm prices by creating artificial scarcity. FSRC agents purchased surplus crops and livestock, which were then distributed to the needy through local charities—killing two birds with one stone, so to speak. In January 1934, for example, the FSRC paid $3.5 million for 234,600 hogs, which were "processed and distributed among the needy unemployed throughout the country."

In its first year, the FSRC distributed to the hungry 259 million pounds of pork, 117 million pounds of canned beef, 23 million pounds of lard, 56 million pounds of butter, 144 million pounds of flour, 20 million pounds of cereal, 7 million pounds of beans, and 885,350 pounds of dried apples. It was a lot of food. Farm prices rose. Farmers were happy. Millions of hungry Americans were fed.

But retailers were furious. To them, the FSRC was unfair competition. The FSRC was a federally funded nonprofit corporation whose charter granted it the power to "purchase or otherwise acquire, hold, own, mortgage, sell, convey, or otherwise dispose of real and personal property of every class, nature, or description." In other words, the FSRC could buy or sell literally anything. Its board of directors included Henry Wallace, the agriculture secretary whose communist sympathies were widely suspected, and Harry Hopkins, a New York liberal and one of FDR's closest advisors, who, as "federal relief administrator," was responsible for implementing the New Deal from top to bottom.

The scope of the FSRC's mandate and the radical bent of its directors terrified the country's capitalists. The FSRC had license to bend if not break the laws of supply and demand. In the fall of 1934 the government announced plans to open a huge "goods exchange" or "commissary" in Tennessee to distribute free food directly to the needy. Grocers nation-wide cried foul. In a letter to Harry Hopkins, the Utah Retail Grocers Association complained that the commissaries would be an "unnecessary infringement on private business and direct competition." In a telegram to President Roosevelt, Tennessee grocers called the proposal "unsound and unethical" and claimed a commissary proposed for Nashville would put one hundred grocery stores out of business.

The head of the Tennessee Emergency Relief Administration (TERA), Walter L. Simpson, couldn't understand what all the fuss was about. He pointed out that the commissaries would provide food only to people who couldn't afford groceries. "How can we put 100 grocers out of business, when we have never put a single one into business?" Simpson asked. "No one will be permitted to get anything from the Goods Exchange [i.e., the commissary] except persons on the TERA relief rolls. Hence the Exchange will not take any customers away from commercial markets." Nonetheless, the Roosevelt administration yielded to the grocers. The commissary plan was scrapped, and the food stamp program was created—not to feed the hungry, really, but to appease business interests.

Henry Wallace is usually given credit for coming up with the idea, though it was surely the collective product of his young and imagina-tive staff. It was a rather byzantine scheme. Eligible recipients (mainly the unemployed) purchased orange-colored stamps, which could be redeemed at face value for any food products. In addition, recipients also received, for free, blue-colored stamps in an amount equal to half the amount of orange stamps purchased. The blue stamps could be redeemed only to purchase foods that the government declared to be in surplus.

The stamps could be redeemed at any grocery store. Grocers could then exchange all the stamps they received, orange and blue, at any bank for their face value in cash. The banks, in turn, would redeem the stamps with the Treasury.

Wallace unveiled the plan at a meeting of the National Food and Grocery Conference Committee in Washington in March 1939. "If this plan is fully successful, it means that the day is not far distant when all the people of the United States will be adequately nourished," Wallace told the committee. "Shortage of vitamin-rich food is in my opinion, responsible for more sickness and lack of abounding, joyous energy in the United States than the various kinds of preventable diseases." Wallace also hoped the plan would solve a perplexing contradiction of the late Depression: "The conscience of the American people has long been shocked by the paradox of farmers impoverished by abundance while at the same time millions of consumers were hungry for food which was rotting because the price for it would not pay the cost of harvesting and transportation."

The food stamp program seemed to be a work of political genius. It would increase grocery sales by an estimated $250 million a year—about a 3 percent increase—and it would satisfy three large and important constituencies: the farmers, who would see their surplus crops purchased by the government and their prices artificially inflated; the grocers, who would see their sales increase; and the hungry, who would be fed.

But not everyone was enamored of the idea, especially on the far right. For the government to compete directly with private enterprise was bad enough; for the government to, in effect, nationalize a private business was even worse. "The plan would seem to point toward ultimate distribution of all food to everybody by this Government device," the reactionary newspaper columnist Mark Sullivan wrote. "Will the time come when the grocer is a Government clerk in a Government-owned shop?"

But the grocers were unconcerned. Food stamps would be good for business. The grocers' committee unanimously endorsed the program, which would be implemented by the Federal Surplus Relief Corporation (which had recently been renamed the Federal Surplus Commodities Corporation). Wallace immediately announced that the program would be tested in five medium-sized cities.

The first would be Rochester, New York. So, early on a dreary Tuesday morning in May 1939, several dozen people lined up outside the Old Post Office on Fitzhugh Street in downtown Rochester. At the front of the line was a thirty-six-year-old unemployed machinist named Ralston Thayer. When the doors were unlocked at nine o'clock, Taylor strode into the imposing brown sandstone building and approached one of the clerks standing behind a long counter. He placed four one-dollar bills on the counter. The clerk handed Thayer several small booklets filled with orange and blue stamps. Ralston Thayer, a proud veteran of the Great War, was the first person in American history to receive food stamps.

For the four dollars he plunked down on the counter, Thayer was given four dollars' worth of orange stamps and two dollars' worth of blue stamps. With the orange stamps he could buy any foods he desired. With the blue stamps, however, he could buy only what was deemed in surplus at the time: butter, eggs, flour, beans, citrus fruits, and cornmeal.

After he claimed his booklets, Thayer was ambushed by newspaper reporters eager for a juicy quote from the nation's first food stamp recipient. They were disappointed. Undoubtedly self-conscious, he proved less than loquacious. "I never got surplus foods before, but I certainly will now," he said. "The plan seems simple enough."

Other recipients were more expansive. "Fried potatoes, onions and coffee made up our best supper for two years," a "32-year-old mother of a typical Rochester relief family" told a local reporter in August. "Now we have eggs, butter, fresh tomatoes, peaches, and pears on the table almost every night."

Rochester grocers were equally ecstatic. By early December, the federal government had already sold more than $1 million worth of orange stamps, meaning more than $500,000 worth of "free" blue stamps had been doled out—and pumped directly into the city's twelve hundred grocery stores. It was, in effect, a welfare program for the city's retailers.

The food stamp program proved so successful in Rochester and the four other test cities (Birmingham, Dayton, Des Moines, and Seattle) that it was rolled out in dozens of cities by the end of the year and expanded to include low-wage workers (the heads of households who earned $19.50 a week or less). By the end of 1940, the program was operating in nearly half the nation's counties. It was phased out during the Second World War because, according to the Department of Agriculture, "the conditions that brought the program into being—unmarketable food surpluses and widespread unemployment—no longer existed." The once-mighty Federal Surplus Commodities Corporation was likewise dissolved, its extraordinary powers no longer deemed necessary.

After witnessing rural poverty firsthand while campaigning in West Virginia, President Kennedy revived the food stamp program shortly after taking office in 1961. The new program eliminated the special stamps for surplus foods—but recipients were still required to purchase their stamps, which now came in denominations of one dollar, five dollars, and ten dollars. The price that recipients paid for the stamps varied based on factors such as age, income, and family size.

The purchase requirement proved onerous to the poorest families. And that's what Swango Fugate told Robert Kennedy at the hearing inside the one-room school in Vortex:

> SENATOR KENNEDY: Has the food stamp program been effective,
> do you think?
> SWANGO FUGATE: Well, here is the point about it, my way look-
> ing at it: I have to pay rent, and of course food stamps
> costs me seventy-two dollars a month, we get ninety-four
> dollars, and I can't pay my rent out of the food stamps,
> and I give him the money, and what am I going to pay
> my rent with? I work on this Unemployed Fathers Job.
> KENNEDY: What do you think should be done?
> FUGATE: I believe they should be cut down.
> KENNEDY: The amount of money you have to pay for the food
> stamps?

FUGATE: That's right.

KENNEDY: How much do you have to pay for them?

FUGATE: Seventy-two dollars, and get ninety-four dollars.

KENNEDY: Seventy-two dollars for your food stamps?

FUGATE: That's right.

KENNEDY: How many in the family?

FUGATE: I've got four boys.

KENNEDY: How old are they?

FUGATE: One is nineteen, fifteen, twelve, and eleven—one boy in Thailand.

KENNEDY: What is he in?

FUGATE: He's a special in that . . .

KENNEDY: Is he in the armed forces? In the army?

FUGATE: Yeah.

KENNEDY: And do the other boys that live at home, do they go to school?

FUGATE: One finished last year and the other three is in school.

KENNEDY: Are there enough jobs around for young men?

FUGATE: No.

KENNEDY: What kind of jobs do they find?

FUGATE: If a young man in our country finds a job he has to leave there. He can't find no job.

KENNEDY: No jobs at all?

FUGATE: No. When he finishes high school there ain't no job for him; if he gets a job he has to leave there.

KENNEDY: Are there any federal job training programs?

FUGATE: Yes.

KENNEDY: What happens to the men that finish these job training programs?

FUGATE: Well, I'm on that job myself, and I have been on it twenty-five months. At the end of my thirty-six months, I'm sixty years old, what benefit will that do to me, a training job? Of course these young men, I don't know.

KENNEDY: What happens to the young men that work—go to the job training program—where do they find jobs?

FUGATE: If they get a job they have to leave.

KENNEDY: There are no jobs available?

FUGATE: No. I did work in the mines a long time but the mines
worked out I was working in and after that I couldn't get
a job.

The fact that food stamps were too expensive for some recipients
was not exactly breaking news to Kennedy. He'd heard about the problem when he toured the Mississippi Delta the previous year, and he'd
asked agriculture secretary Orville Freeman to do something about it.
Freeman agreed to lower the purchase price for the poorest food stamp
recipients. Evidently, however, prices were still too high for some.

10

Black and Proud

THE OTHER NOTABLE WITNESS AT the one-room schoolhouse in Vortex that cold February afternoon was Mary Rice Farris, the only African American to testify at the hearing that day. She was a formidable woman. Tirelessly active in politics, her community, and her church, she would, her granddaughter Michele Farris recalls, fly to Washington for meetings with government officials, then fly back home, "change clothes and work in tobacco fields, tend to the animals, cook and keep house as a farmer's wife without missing a beat."

Mary Rice was born in Berea, Kentucky, on January 13, 1914. Her mother was a black woman named Mattie Rice. Her father was a white man named Harrison Kinnard, who was in his sixties when Mary was born and was married to another woman. Mary's light skin made her biracial parentage apparent, but, according to her granddaughter, she never embraced her white heritage. "She was ashamed that the word 'illegitimate' was on her birth certificate," Michele Farris tells me. "She'd say, 'I'm black and I'm proud.'"

Mary attended Lincoln Institute, an all-black high school, and in 1931, when she was seventeen, married a tobacco farmer named Moss Farris. They lived on a farm in a part of Berea known as Farristown, a predominantly African American community named for one of Farris's ancestors. Mary and Moss had four children and worked hard to provide for them. Besides burley tobacco, they grew potatoes and beans and operated a small dairy farm. They also kept pigs and chickens, and Moss trained Tennessee Walking Horses for wealthy white sponsors. His favorite was named Lucky.

Mary worked a series of jobs away from the farm to help make ends meet. For many years she was the "night hostess" at the women's dormitory at Eastern Kentucky University, and in that role she mentored hundreds of young women. "They loved her dearly," Michele Farris says, "some staying up all night to talk to her about their problems and receive motherly advice. She loved to see young people have a good clean time and also brought them along with her on many of her adventures so their eyes would be open to the world. Her goal was to make life better for all people."

The stereotypical Appalachian is always white, and the myth of what the historian Aaron Astor calls the "whitened archetype of Appalachia" is as tenacious as it is pernicious. In fact, African Americans comprised between 14 and 19 percent of Appalachia's population in the nineteenth century and between 9 and 13 percent in the twentieth, and today still make up between 9 and 10 percent of the population. African Americans were crucial to Appalachia's economic and cultural development. They mined the coal and tilled the fields. From Africa they imported a musical instrument that has come to embody traditional Appalachian music: the banjo. And, like Mary Rice Farris, they played key roles in social movements and were leaders in their communities.

Mary worked closely with Volunteers in Service to America (VISTA) in Madison County and, like Swango Fugate, helped manage a large OEO grant for antipoverty programs. And, while her husband, Moss, was a loyal Democrat, Mary was a lifelong Republican. Born less than fifty years after the end of the Civil War, she identified closely with the party of Lincoln. She was the chairperson of the local Republican committee and a poll watcher on election days. Local politicians—always white—of both parties never failed to call on her before an election, as her endorsement was key to winning votes in Farristown. Mary Farris was a fundamentalist when it came to religion—she was a devout Baptist—and the right to vote. "She made sure those that did not have transportation were able to vote," Michele Farris says. "She would always say that we as black people should exercise our right to vote. It was not given to us. People fought and died so we could vote."

Through her father, Mary qualified for membership in the Daughters of the American Revolution, but the organization did not begin admitting African Americans until 1977—the year she died. It would have been an appropriate honor. "She was a sweet, lovely woman," Michele Farris tells me, "but she was a natural-born fighter." It's no surprise, then, that when she was given the opportunity to testify at the hearing in the one-room schoolhouse in Vortex, she pulled no punches. In fact, she turned the tables on Senator Kennedy and Congressman Perkins and began her testimony by asking them questions that clearly made them uncomfortable.

> MARY RICE FARRIS: Senator, Mr. Perkins: If we are spending $70 million a day* in Vietnam, plus loss of life, when there are millions of people in our area hungry, without homes and decent housing, or without clothing—and we would also like to know why the Negro is having to fight, too, for a decent place in society as a rightful American citizen?
>
> SENATOR KENNEDY: You have turned this hearing around. You are asking us questions.
>
> FARRIS: I want an answer and then you ask me.
>
> KENNEDY [to Carl Perkins]: Are you listening, Congressman? [Kennedy smiles]

Even reading the transcript, the condescension is palpable. The senator and the congressman addressed the other five witnesses at Vortex that day as either "Mr." or "Mrs." but bestowed no such honorific on Mary Rice Farris. At one point, Perkins referred to her dismissively as "this lady here." Her pointed questions clearly irked the two members of Congress. There is a sense that they wished she knew her place, that they were taken aback by what they considered her impertinence and were uncomfortable being questioned by a poor black woman. That's not how things worked in their world.

---

* The figure was actually closer to $200 million a day.

Mary Rice Farris, circa 1968. *Michele Farris*

But she was already in her place, at the center of her community, and when racial unrest visited Berea later that year, Mary Rice Farris would be called upon to help bridge the divide between blacks and whites. The unrest was stoked by a stocky fifty-five-year-old white man with an unlikely nickname: Reverend Connie.

11

Reverend Connie

ON THE AFTERNOON OF SUNDAY, SEPTEMBER 1, 1968, about three hundred white people—mostly men—gathered at a vacant used-car lot on US 25 in Berea for a rally and fundraiser sponsored by the National States' Rights Party (NSRP). It was a lovely late-summer day, with clear skies and highs in the upper seventies. It was a holiday weekend too: the day before Labor Day.

The crowd was in high spirits, so to speak, when Charles Conley Lynch was introduced as the featured speaker. Lynch liked to be called Connie—a diminutive of his middle name. He was a handsome man, with a dimpled chin and a penchant for wearing Kentucky Colonel ties. He was also an unrepentant racist, a minister ordained in the Church of Jesus Christ–Christian, a Christian Identity sect founded in 1946 by the Ku Klux Klan organizer and Holocaust denier Wesley A. Swift. One of Swift's acolytes was Richard Butler, who would take over the church after Swift died in 1971 and merge it with a new organization Butler founded in Idaho, the Aryan Nations.*

Another Swift acolyte was Charles Conley Lynch. Lynch was born in 1912 in the East Texas town of Clarksville, near the Oklahoma border.

---

* According to the Christian Identity movement, only so-called Aryans are the true descendants of the ancient Israelites. Virulently racist and anti-Semitic, as well as completely divorced from historical and biological reality, the movement believes all nonwhites must be enslaved or exterminated in order to bring about a heavenly kingdom on earth for whites only.

His parents were poor cotton farmers. During the Depression, Lynch moved to Southern California, where he found work picking fruit and building houses. He joined the Church of Jesus Christ–Christian in the 1940s, and after the Supreme Court's 1954 *Brown* decision outlawing segregated schools, he became an itinerant rabble rouser, living out of his car as he traveled the country preaching his gospel of hate. Lynch appeared on the sidelines of the era's most explosive racial confrontations: Little Rock, Oxford, Birmingham. He was often accompanied by another gadfly racist, an Atlanta lawyer named Jesse Benjamin "J. B." Stoner, a founder of the NSRP. In 1980 Stoner would be convicted of the 1958 bombing of a black church in Birmingham, Alabama. "Lynch and Stoner made a macabre double act at Klan rallies," noted Clive Webb in *Rabble Rousers: The American Far Right in the Civil Rights Era*, "trading the microphone with one another as they stirred their audiences into frenzies."

In the summer of 1965, Lynch and Stoner made their way to Anniston, Alabama, where they held rallies on the courthouse steps for three nights in July. During these rallies, according to the *Anniston Star*, Lynch advocated "violence and murder." He did not couch his racism in euphemism. "If it takes killing to get the Negroes out of the white men's streets and to protect our constitutional rights," he was reported to have said at the rally on the evening of Thursday, July 15, "I say, yes, kill them."

Riding home from the rally in a beat-up '55 Chevy that night, three friends—Clarence Lewis Blevins, Johnny Ira DeFries, and Hubert Damon Strange, all in their twenties—decided to follow Lynch's counsel. Around 11:30, they came up behind a car on Highway 202. Inside were four black men coming home from their shifts at the Alabama Pipe Company. Strange leaned out the passenger window with a shotgun and fired three times at the car, blowing out the rear window. The driver, thirty-eight-year-old Willie Brewster, was wounded in the neck. The other three men in the car were not seriously injured. Later that night DeFries bragged to a friend, "We got us a nigger."

Willie Brewster died three days later, leaving behind his wife, thirty-one-year-old Lestine, and their two children, a five-year-old boy and a four-year-old girl. Lestine was pregnant with their third child. She would miscarry less than two weeks later.

The murder galvanized whites in Anniston, but not in the way Connie Lynch expected. Civic leaders, including the mayor, police chief, and county commissioners, pitched in to raise a $20,000 reward for information leading to the arrest and conviction of those responsible for the shooting. The generous reward—about $145,000 in today's money—pricked the conscience of the friend to whom Johnny DeFries had bragged on the night of the shooting. He contacted the authorities, who arrested DeFries and his two accomplices in late August. Damon Strange, the triggerman, was the first to be tried. His lawyer was none other than J. B. Stoner, who predicted a swift acquittal, but an all-white jury found Strange guilty of second-degree murder. It was, the *Washington Post* noted, "the first time in modern times that a white man had been convicted of murder in the Deep South for the racial slaying of a Negro." When the verdict was announced, Strange "turned white" and Stoner began to cry. (Strange was sentenced to ten years in prison. DeFries, the driver of the car that night, was later found not guilty of murder. The charges against Lewis Blevins were dropped.)

With local resistance to their hate campaigns in the Deep South mounting, Lynch and Stoner began looking north for followers and funds. The National States' Rights Party established a chapter in Dayton, Ohio, and in the summer of 1968 the party scheduled recruitment rallies in Indianapolis, Indiana; Fort Mitchell, Kentucky; Lexington, Kentucky; and Berea, Kentucky. An article in the party's newspaper, the *Thunderbolt*, said a July 20 event in Berea was "well received." Six weeks later, the NSRP returned to Berea.

The rally on September 1 was routine, insofar as a white supremacy rally can be routine. Reverend Connie fired up the crowd with his usual incendiary rhetoric—"anti-Negro talk," as the papers put it the next day. George Wallace's third-party campaign for president, in full bloom two months before the election, was enthusiastically endorsed.

By four o'clock the rally was over. The organizers were packing away their placards, flyers, and Confederate flags when "several carloads of Negro men" pulled up to the site. Words, including racial epithets, were exchanged. Then the shooting began. Over the next ten minutes, the two sides exchanged more than forty shots in a running gun battle. When the smoke cleared, two men—one white and one black—were dead and several others were wounded.*

The Berea City Council held an emergency session the next day, Labor Day. Mary Rice Farris was in attendance—and angry. She demanded to know why the city had allowed the rally to take place. "If we'd had a civil rights meeting," she told the council, "we would have been surrounded by police." She said the council had been "complacent as far as we (Negroes) are concerned, and we've let you get away with it. We don't want to make demands but there are things that need to be done." She pointedly noted that the town's mayor and eight councilmen were all white.

Only about two hundred of Berea's forty-three hundred residents were black, and most lived in neighborhoods scattered on the outskirts of town. It was a long way from Watts, Newark, or Detroit, but Berea's black residents faced many of the same indignities, large and small, as well as the institutional racism, that the residents of those urban ghettoes

---

* The white victim was Elza V. Rucker, thirty, an NSRP "sergeant-at-arms" and father of three. The black victim was thirty-six-year-old Lenoa John Boggs, a presser at Sav-Way Cleaners and father of five. They are buried less than one hundred yards apart in Berea Cemetery. Rucker's eight-year-old daughter was at the rally and witnessed his murder. She tells me her father got involved with the NSRP through his father-in-law, who was an associate of J. B. Stoner (whom she describes as "the devil himself"). Her father, she says, was brainwashed—he wasn't even 100 percent white, she says; he was part Cherokee. She also says she abhors racism and now "follow[s] the Jewish faith." I ask her if she has converted to Judaism and she says she was "grafted in."

Six black men were charged with Rucker's murder. The charges were later reduced to unlawful assembly. The six men pleaded guilty and were sentenced to nine months in jail.

Eight white men were charged with Boggs's murder. Charges against two were dropped. The charges against the other six—including Lynch—were reduced to disorderly conduct. All but Lynch—who was already serving a sentence in a Maryland prison for inciting a riot in Baltimore—were tried in March 1969. Their lawyer was J. B. Stoner. The five were found guilty and were fined $500 each. Three of the five were also sentenced to thirty days in jail. The inequity of the sentences did not go unnoticed in Berea's black community.

faced. Whites in Berea routinely referred to black men as "boys." "The Negro boys were goaded into it by the States Rights people," Mayor Clint Hensley said after the shoot-out. "I know every one of them (the Negroes) and they are good boys." (The youngest of the six black men arrested was thirty.) "I hate to see things like that happen," a white gas station attendant told a reporter. "He"—Lenoa John Boggs, the black man killed in the shoot-out—"was a fine boy, one of our best." (Boggs, remember, was thirty-six.)

Black men also found it difficult to find work at Berea College, the town's largest employer. Michele Farris tells me her grandfather—Mary's husband, Moss Farris—was never able to get hired by the school, even for janitorial work, although he was "an inventor and mechanic who could build or fix anything." The college was also criticized for its slow pace of integration. Founded in 1855 by abolitionists committed to inter-racial education, the college was forced by a state law to stop admitting black students in 1904. The law was repealed in 1950, but in 1968 blacks made up just 5 percent of the student body, and not a single faculty member was black. "We've been scouring the earth trying to find some," the college's president, Willis Weatherford Jr., told the city council.

"Townspeople seem benevolent toward the Negro," an Associated Press reporter who visited Berea in the days after the shooting wrote, "saying over and over that he should 'stay in his place,' but shouldn't suffer indignities of 'outside agitators.'"

At the end of the emergency session, the Berea City Council adopted a resolution blaming the National States' Rights Party for its "provocative action which disturbed a century of good feelings between members of both races in the Berea area." The council also authorized the formation of a special commission on race relations. Mary Rice Farris was asked to serve on the commission and accepted.

In October 1968 Farris was invited to speak at a forum on race relations hosted by Berea College. Her speech was reminiscent of Robert Kennedy's famous remarks in Indianapolis on the night Martin Luther King Jr. was murdered, when he said, "What we need in the United States is not division; what we need in the United States is not hatred; what we need in the United States is not violence or lawlessness; but love and wisdom, and compassion toward one another, and a feeling of justice toward those who still suffer within our country, whether they be white or they be black." Kennedy was a white man addressing a largely black audience. Farris was addressing an auditorium filled with college students, nearly all white:

> It is true, both white and negro want change—change is inevitable—one way or another. Let's face the fact that irresponsible, erratic, violent change is illogical, unreasonable and un-spiritual, and will only lead to utter chaos. We as Christians have to remember we operate from unchanging foundations. In God there is no Jew or Greek, male or female. Of one blood God has created all men. Jesus in his stay on Earth broke the racial zones of Gentile and the Samaritan. He said, "If a man say, I love God, and hateth his brother, he is a liar: for he that loveth not his brother whom he hath seen, how can he love God whom he hath not seen?"

Neither Senator Kennedy nor Congressman Perkins ever got around to answering Mary Farris's questions at the schoolhouse hearing. After Kennedy facetiously asked Perkins if he was listening, Perkins told Farris, "I'll get around to you." When he finally did—after calling on the other five witnesses first—he said, "Now, this lady, here, I do not have the answers to her questions, so that's it."

But Farris was unfazed. She turned to Kennedy and asked again, "Senator Kennedy, could you give me some answer about the Vietnam situation? Our boys are getting killed and dollars spent on it, and people are hungry, don't have decent clothing, and why we, as American Negroes, are having to fight and speak out for a right to take decent responsibility in this great nation?"

Kennedy urged her to submit her questions to him in writing. Then the hearing ended. Notably, despite her pointed questions, Mary Rice Farris was not mentioned in any of the stories about the hearing that appeared in the next day's newspapers. Later that month, however, her words reached a national audience. In its February 29 issue, the popular black-oriented magazine *Jet*—"The Weekly Negro News

Magazine"—included an excerpt from Farris's testimony in its weekly roundup of notable quotes, Words of the Week:

> **Mary Rice Farris**, a VISTA volunteer, to Sen. Robert F. Kennedy (D., N.Y.) when he spoke to some 150 poor white people in Campton, Ky., *"We want to know why we are spending $7 million [sic] a day in Vietnam, but are still not getting enough food stamps in Appalachia."*

Two of the other notable African Americans quoted on that page: Arthur Ashe and Martin Luther King Jr.

12

Just Pee in This Jug

FROM VORTEX, KENNEDY'S CARAVAN made its way south on Route 15, passing through a series of towns—Bethany, Vancleve, Quicksand, Haddix, Lost Creek—stopping at homes along the road occasionally to chat with residents. A long line of reporters followed in their own automobiles, creating chaotic and comical scenes whenever Kennedy stopped. When Peter Edelman was planning the trip, he had underestimated the interest it would generate. "It wasn't because everybody wanted to see hunger in eastern Kentucky," he explains. "They wanted to know whether he was gonna run for president."

By now—February 13, 1968—it was apparent that Kennedy was seriously considering challenging Lyndon Johnson for the Democratic nomination, notwithstanding his standard and oft-repeated half denial: "I have no plans to run." Minnesota senator Eugene McCarthy was running a credible campaign against Johnson in New Hampshire; a month later, on March 12, he would win a shocking 42 percent of the vote in the state's primary (never mind that Johnson barely campaigned).

"We didn't get a bus [for the press], which we should've done," Edelman says. "We got a little blindsided and were a little dumb. We were thinking in Kentucky we'll get like five reporters, some local reporters, it's not a big deal. But out in the real world at this particular time there's a lot of speculation about whether he's gonna throw his hat in the ring. So it turns out something like thirty-five cars [were following

Kennedy] and so what happened, we get to the house and we would get out of the car and the first few press people would get there. They couldn't all get in the house anyway even if they'd been in a bus. But we would go in and the first few reporters would get in the house and they'd have a nice conversation and get done and they'd get in the car and 80 to 90 percent of the reporters were just pulling up. It was funny but those reporters were very annoyed!"

In a gesture of vehicular bipartisanship, Kentucky's recently inaugurated Republican governor, Louie Nunn, had provided Kennedy free use of a state-owned car, a Chrysler Imperial, as well as a state trooper to act as his driver. Considering Kennedy's brother had been assassinated just over four years earlier, the security arrangements for the trip were surprisingly relaxed. The state trooper acted as Kennedy's de facto bodyguard, but otherwise no special precautions were taken. "We had no concerns about security," Edelman says.

Riding along in the car with Kennedy and Congressman Perkins that day was a twenty-four-year-old University of Kentucky law student named Steve Cawood, who vividly remembers one stop. "[Kennedy] reached over and grabbed the driver and said stop. He jumped out of the car and ran down this little dirt road to a shack of a place, and there was one old Chevrolet up on jacks and three or four of the same model of Chevrolet junked, sitting there in this fella's grubby yard and a couple of men working on the one on jacks. And as he jumped out of the car he said, 'That's exactly my point, that's exactly what I'm trying to prove!' And we had no earthly idea what he was trying to prove, but when he came back to the car he said, 'Those fellas were robbing those old cars they'd bought for twenty-five dollars apiece and they were pulling the parts off those to make this one run so he could drive to work. And that proves these people want to work!'

"The whole time I was in the car with him he was like a damn machine, just constantly asking one question after another, and you could just hear the wheels clicking, and I was so impressed. And I instantly knew there was nobody else running for the presidency that could understand what those fellas were doing over there with those old junk cars. No one that would've had that understanding and empathy—instant empathy—instant grasp of what poor people went through every day. And I became a true believer."

How did Steve Cawood come to occupy such a prominent place in the Kennedy caravan, riding in the same car with the senator and Congressman Perkins? The answer is a mystery—even to him. "When I heard about it [Kennedy's trip to eastern Kentucky], I guarantee you I was head over heels, and I jumped at the opportunity to insert myself into it," Cawood tells me one warm summer morning in 2018. We are sitting on the porch of his home in Pineville, Bell County, on the western edge of eastern Kentucky's coalfields, just north of the Cumberland Gap and the Tennessee state line. Cawood's English setter, Daisy, sits curled at his feet. Cawood speaks softly, and the symphony of cicadas in his yard threatens to drown him out. "I doubt they said, well, we hear Steve Cawood's a bright leader or something." Cawood speculates that Perkins may have had a hand in getting him invited to ride along in Kennedy's car. After all, Cawood and Perkins had already spent many hours together traveling by automobile, and the congressman clearly found the law student to be an amiable travel companion.

Steve Cawood, photographed at his home in Pineville, Kentucky, February 2019. *Lou Murrey*

"I worshipped Carl Perkins," Cawood tells me. "During that period of '66 to '68, I would go to Washington to raise money [for antipoverty programs], and I'd go up there for a meeting in the middle of the week, and it would end up Perkins would ask me to drive him home. He would drive home on Thursday night or Friday morning from Washington to Hindman in an old beat-up '54 or '55 Chevrolet coupe. And he and I would talk politics all the way from Washington home.

"I can remember, he'd carry a great big ol' thermos of coffee in the front seat, hand me a damn gallon milk jug and tell me, 'If you need to pee, you just pee in this jug and we'll pour it out the window.' And we'd go down US 11 out of Washington.

"Perkins was really behind Bobby and wanted to see him run [for president], and I may have connected [with Kennedy's staff] through Carl Perkins."

However he ended up there, the backseat of Robert Kennedy's car was a lofty perch for a kid from Pineville. Cawood was born in 1943, the oldest of three children. His parents were descended from early white settlers in Kentucky. His maternal grandfather, James M. Gilbert, was a circuit court judge. "My family was lower middle class," Cawood tells me. "My mother always worked. There were three or four hardware stores in Pineville at the time. My dad's was the small one. We didn't take vacations or anything of that sort. But I was never poor. We always had something to eat. We had a house my dad and mother owned."

To attract customers, Steve's dad ran a coaxial cable from an antenna high up on Pine Mountain to a television set in the front window of his hardware store. It didn't do much to improve sales, but a small crowd was always camped on the sidewalk in front of the store, watching the snowy pictures from stations in distant and exotic locales like Johnson City, Tennessee.

The Pineville that Cawood grew up in was a comfortable if somewhat isolated town of thirty-five hundred, wedged in between Pine Mountain and a big bend on the Cumberland River. Every May the town hosted (and still hosts) the Kentucky Mountain Laurel Festival, a celebration of Appalachian culture and "Southern hospitality." It was almost idyllic.

Almost, because just outside town lived Cawood's friends whose fathers worked the mines and whose lives were considerably more difficult than his own. As he grew up, he began to realize that the world outside Pineville's sheltered 1.7 square miles was more complicated than he'd first believed. "At that time in a small town like Pineville it could be a misleading experience to live in the town as opposed to five miles out of town." He began reading about the history of his home. "When I was growing up, I never heard a thing about the brutality of the labor organizing here, and when I began to read and learn what had occurred here it was just a kind of a dawning on me that things were as bad as they were."

Things were very bad indeed for the miners who lived outside Pineville during the long winter of 1930–31. With the Depression deepening and the demand for coal plummeting, mine operators in the Harlan coalfields, which cover parts of Bell, Harlan, and Knox Counties, cut their workers' wages by 10 percent, from $5.00 a day to $4.50.

Coal mining was dirty, dangerous work, and a miner's life was completely circumscribed by his company: He was forced to rent a company house, and to buy his food and clothing, at inflated prices, at the company store. If he was arrested, he spent time in a company jail. The mines controlled every aspect of a miner's life and, by extension, every aspect of the county's civic life.

The workers responded to the wage cut with outrage—and strikes. Miners who refused to work—and their families—were banished from company homes in the middle of winter. Hunger was rampant. The miners were not unionized, so organizers from the United Mine Workers of America moved into the region. Hundreds of miners in the Harlan coalfields joined the UMWA that winter, demanding higher wages and better working conditions. On March 1, 1931, more than two thousand miners from Bell and Harlan Counties attended a UMWA rally at the Pineville theater. The mine operators, however, refused to recognize the union.

The operators believed unionization would lead inevitably to bankruptcy. Mines in the northern coalfields of western Pennsylvania, eastern Ohio, and northern West Virginia could ship their coal to eastern markets much more cheaply than the mines in the remote mountains of eastern Kentucky, where railroads were scattered and expensive. The eastern Kentucky mines had one competitive advantage, however: unlike the unionized mines up north, they paid low wages. If their mines were unionized, the operators feared, wages would rise and their only competitive advantage would vanish. They would be forced out of business. In fact, many mine operators in eastern Kentucky believed the drive to unionize their mines was secretly organized by their competitors in the North.

Doing the mine operators' bidding, county sheriffs deputized scores of strikebreakers, all of whom were paid by the mines, not the county. These "private deputies" roamed the coalfields, intimidating and harassing striking workers and their families. In other words, they were mercenaries. "Their substantial criminal records and unsavory reputations as gunmen merited the miners' characterization of them as gun thugs," wrote John W. Hevener in *Which Side Are You On?*, his history of the Harlan Mine Wars. Harlan County sheriff John Henry Blair supervised 170 deputies, only about six of whom were paid by the county. The rest were on mine company payrolls. Blair was unapologetic about taking sides. "I did all in my power to aid the coal operators," he later said. "There was no compromise when labor troubles swept the county and the 'Reds' came into Harlan County."

The wide availability of firearms made violent clashes between the striking miners and the private deputies inevitable. A 1932 study estimated that one in five Harlan County residents carried a pistol. And they weren't afraid to use them; in the 1920s, the county's homicide rate was an astonishing 77.6 per 100,000 residents, higher than any other county in the nation and twice as high as the rate in Florida, the most murderous state.*

---

* The homicide rate in Harlan County today is 6 per 100,000, more than 20 percent above the national average of 4.9. (From 2009 to 2015 the county with the highest homicide rate was Orleans Parish, Louisiana, which encompasses New Orleans, with an annual average of 43 per 100,000.) Why was Harlan County's homicide rate so high in the early decades of the twentieth century? It's a question that has long confounded sociologists. Numerous theories have been floated: poverty, race, a history of feuding, high rates of gun ownership, the prevalence of "low-status" jobs, the rural character of the place. But to many

The striking miners waged a guerrilla war against the mine operators. They blew up mine shafts, tipples, and mining equipment. And, on
the morning of Tuesday, May 5, 1931, they ambushed a convoy of the
hated private deputies. Three cars carrying ten deputies were on their
way from Verda to the company town of Kenvir (named for its location near the Kentucky-Virginia border). Between fifty and seventy-five
miners, tipped off about the motorcade, lay in wait, hidden among the
trees lining the road just outside Evarts. As the cars approached, the
miners unleashed a ferocious volley of rifle and shotgun fire. The deputies stopped and returned fire. By the time the shoot-out ended thirty
minutes later, an estimated one thousand rounds had been exchanged.
Three of the deputies were dead. Two were wounded. One of the miners
was also dead. Forty-three union miners would eventually be charged
in connection with the deaths of the three deputies.

The Battle of Evarts, as it came to be known, galvanized the miners.
In the week following the shoot-out, the number of miners on strike
in the Harlan coalfields ballooned from eighteen hundred to fifty-eight
hundred. At the behest of the mine operators, Kentucky governor Flem
Sampson ordered the National Guard to the coalfields, ostensibly to
restore order. Believing the troops would protect them from retaliation
by the hated deputies, the striking miners greeted them with a parade
in Evarts on May 7. But it soon became apparent that the guard's real
purpose was to end the strike. Working with the private deputies, guard
troops violently broke up picket lines and union meetings. Public assem-
blies were banned, in clear violation of the First Amendment.

Hunger among the strikers and their families worsened. They
appealed to the Red Cross for help, but the organization refused, citing
a policy forbidding it from intervening in a labor dispute. "Why we must
have a policy," explained Red Cross Bell County chairman Herndon
Evans, who was also the editor of the *Pineville Sun* and owned shares
in "a mine or two." "We have to check up whether people deserve help
or not, and of course we call the operators to know whether a miner

---

researchers the most persuasive theory was proposed by the historian Sheldon Hackney,
who found a correlation between high homicide rates and low levels of education. In 1930,
10.6 percent of Harlan County's population over ten years of age was illiterate.

who asks for help has been working or not," Evans said. "We can't encourage the strike. . . . We made it a policy—a local policy, whether it is in conformity with the national organization or not—when men on strike came to us for aid, to turn them down because of limited funds."

The UMWA, facing bankruptcy, was unable to offer material support. The miners turned to the National Guard for help, but the commanding officer, Colonel Dan Carrell, dismissed their pleas, telling the hungry miners they could expect "absolutely no help" as long as they remained on strike. "If we cannot get help from anyone else we are going to help ourselves," warned the local UMWA president William Hightower, an illiterate seventy-seven-year-old miner who had been fired from the Harlan-Wallis Coal Corporation for his union activity. "We are not going to let our families starve."

The miners found little support in the towns, where, according to the communist historian Oakley Johnson, "a highly conservative combination of governmental and mine-owning forces" were arrayed against them. A few sympathetic locals, however, offered the striking miners what little support they could. Joe Cawood—Steve's great-uncle—owned a grocery store in Evarts. According to one account, he was "among the most generous provisioners" during the strike. Cawood had won the Republican primary for Harlan County sheriff in August 1929, but his name was not on the ballot for the general election that November, due to a rival faction of Republicans, who supported John Henry Blair for sheriff, bringing accusations of election fraud against Cawood, a charge he vehemently denied. In an audacious case of electoral legerdemain, even by the standards of eastern Kentucky, the Blair faction appealed the primary result to circuit court judge Davy Crockett Jones, who ruled that his crony Blair, not Cawood, was the rightful Republican nominee. Cawood's brother, W. P. Cawood—another of Steve's great-uncles—ran against Blair in the general election as an independent candidate. Amid more charges of fraud on both sides, J. H. Blair defeated W. P. Cawood by 155 votes (7,501 to 7,346). If either Cawood brother had prevailed, the notorious J. H. Blair might have been lost to history. Instead he was immortalized in "Which Side Are You On?," a song written by Florence Reece, whose husband was a miner and UMWA organizer, after their home was raided by private deputies. The song would eventually become an anthem of the labor movement, popularized by Pete Seeger and other folk singers.

> They say in Harlan County
> There are no neutrals there
> You'll either be a union man
> Or a thug for J. H. Blair
> Which side are you on?
> Which side are you on?

But support from generous and sympathetic allies could only go so far. Desperate and hungry, striking miners began breaking into company commissaries and grocery stores. The Evarts A&P was broken into three times in a single week. "Ultimately," wrote John W. Hevener, "the miners were to be starved back into the pits." It worked. By the time the National Guard was recalled from the coalfields in late July, fewer than one thousand miners were still on strike.

13

Sedition

THOUGH STILL IN LAW SCHOOL, Steve Cawood was a minor player in a major legal drama unfolding in eastern Kentucky that winter of 1967–68. The case involved several disparate elements, including the War on Poverty, do-gooders, suspicious locals, and, allegedly, a plot to overthrow the government. The government of Pike County, Kentucky, that is.

Robert Kennedy was probably familiar with the case—a story about it had appeared in the *New York Times*—but he never commented on it, and he did not cross paths with the defendants while he was in eastern Kentucky. But the case—which came to be known as *McSurely v. Ratliff*—encapsulates the issues underlying Kennedy's trip, namely poverty, power, and justice.

It all began the previous summer. Alan and Margaret McSurely spent the afternoon of Friday, August 11, 1967, at the home of their friends Joseph and Karen Mulloy in the mountains of Pike County. The two couples had become close through their antipoverty work in the county. The McSurelys worked for a group called the Southern Conference Education Fund. Joe Mulloy was a "field man" for the Appalachian Volunteers, a War on Poverty program funded by the Office of Economic Opportunity in Washington. It was a pleasant, sunny day, with temperatures in the seventies. Al and Joe played basketball while their wives chatted, mostly about Margaret's pregnancy: she was five months along. When it came time for the McSurelys to leave, Karen gave them some summer squash from her garden.

Around seven o'clock that evening, Margaret was in her kitchen cooking the squash when she was alarmed to see about a dozen men with guns outside her window. "My goodness," she remembered thinking to herself, "they must be looking for an escaped convict." When Al opened the front door to investigate, the men burst past him and into the house. One of them was the Pike County sheriff, Perry Justice, who shouted, "Where is Alan McSurely?"

"Right here," answered Al, still standing in the doorway. At six feet, four inches tall, he was hard to miss.

Soon the local state prosecutor, Thomas Ratliff, arrived. He informed the McSurelys that they were under arrest. The charge was sedition. Specifically, they were accused of plotting to overthrow the government of Pike County. He produced a search warrant. Sheriff Justice's deputies were authorized to remove "all printed or handwritten material" in the house. Ratliff pulled a director's chair up to the bookcase in the living room and went through their books one by one, separating them into piles on the floor. "Other men went into the bedroom and took the bed apart," Margaret remembered. "They went through the dresser drawers and the closet. They rooted through Al's desk and boxes of our papers. They just took everything. 'Lookie here, Thomas,' one said, 'the *Village Voice*. That's where all them beatniks are.' It was bizarre, comical, and terribly frightening at the same time."

The deputies ended up confiscating more than five hundred books and more than twenty cardboard boxes filled with pamphlets, flyers, posters, correspondence, and paperwork. Personal effects, including clothing, were confiscated as well. The sheriff had to commandeer a neighbor's pickup truck to haul it all away. Al and Margaret followed in a police car.

Around midnight, the raid was repeated at the Mulloys' home, though only a few boxes of papers were seized. Joe Mulloy was arrested. (Karen Mulloy was not.) Like the McSurelys, he was charged with sedition. All three were detained in the Pike County jail in the county seat, Pikeville.

At a press conference in Pikeville the next day, Ratliff—a million-aire coal operator who also happened to be the Republican candidate for lieutenant governor at the time—said the books seized from the McSurelys comprised a "communistic library out of this world." They included works by and about Lenin, Marx, Mao, Castro, and "other Communist leaders," as well as a collection of Russian short stories and a book about the "so-called Berkeley student revolt." Unmentioned by Ratliff were the books the deputies left behind, including *The Conscience of a Conservative* by Barry Goldwater and the Holy Bible.

Also confiscated, Ratliff announced, was "A New Political Union," a paper written by Al McSurely that, according to the prosecutor/candidate, included plans on how to "take over Pike County from the power structure and put it in the hands of the poor." In the paper, McSurely predicted the 1968 presidential candidates would be Robert Kennedy and Ronald Reagan and the election would be "an intramural football game, arranged by the owners of both teams, to see which team gets to play around with the lives of 96% of American citizens for four years." Due to the "irrelevancy of the ideas and the ineffectiveness of the programs" of the two major political parties, he called for "the organization of a national new political union."

"One must set his goal," McSurely wrote, "determine the theory he is going to operate on, and then *never, never veer* from this path . . . because when the struggle heats up, we must live and die with those ideas and theories we have finally chosen." Milton Ogle, the director of the Appalachian Volunteers, called the paper "totally simple, almost naive," but to prosecutor Thomas Ratliff it was nothing less than a blueprint for violent revolution. "The paper also included a narrative on ways to get into the government's anti-poverty programs and take advantage of the money available through the programs," Ratliff said. "Every piece of evidence we have points to just one objective, to stir up dissension and create turmoil among our poor."

Ratliff claimed that the McSurelys and Mulloy were using government funds "to promote causes aimed at downgrading and maybe overthrowing the government" and that they had "indoctrinated" local youth. He said he would be sharing the confiscated material with the

US Senate committee investigating civil disorder. He also demanded that "the federal government withdraw all anti-poverty funds and all anti-poverty workers from Appalachia at once"—a rather grand demand from a candidate for lieutenant governor of Kentucky.

Ratliff said the authorities were tipped off by James Madison Compton, the McSurelys' former landlord, who said he evicted the couple after witnessing "a parade of strange looking visitors at their house." (The McSurelys had allowed Peace Corps and VISTA volunteers in the area for training to stay with them.) Sheriff Justice—a high school dropout who doubled as the local undertaker—also heard reports of meetings attended by whites and blacks at the McSurelys', which he regarded as prima facie evidence of sedition.

Joe Mulloy was implicated due to his close relationship with the McSurelys. Warrants were obtained to search the two homes for "seditious matter."

The trio were charged with sedition under KRS 432.040, a law passed during the first Red Scare in 1920, which read in part: "It shall be unlawful for any person or persons, by speech, writing or otherwise, to arouse, incite or fix enmity, discord or strife or ill feeling between classes of persons for the purpose of inducing tumult or disorder."

The statute was so broad and vague that even the Republican governor who signed it, Edwin P. Morrow, was skeptical of its constitutionality. "I have signed it because I feel the need of [a] law against those who advise the overthrow of the Government by force," he said, "but with the belief that the courts of the land will take out of this law the sections which make it dangerous."

Thirty-six years later, in 1956, the US Supreme Court ruled that Stjepan Mesaros (called Steve Nelson), a Communist Party official from Pittsburgh, could not be prosecuted for violating Pennsylvania's sedition act. Mesaros, a Croatian American who'd fought against the fascists in the Spanish Civil War, had been arrested after police raided a Communist Party office in Pittsburgh in August 1950. In its six-to-three ruling, the court found that federal sedition laws supersede state sedition statutes. In the majority opinion, Chief Justice Earl Warren noted that Congress had passed three major sedition laws: the Smith Act of 1940, the Internal Security Act of 1950, and the Communist Control Act of 1954. "Congress having thus treated seditious conduct as a matter of vital national concern," Warren wrote, "it is in no sense a local enforcement problem." The ruling effectively struck down the sedition laws in Pennsylvania and forty-one other states—including Kentucky. But in Kentucky, the legislature never bothered to take the law off the books.

Thomas Ratliff knew that the charges against the McSurelys and Mulloy would never stick. He might win convictions in Pike County, but they would certainly be overturned on appeal. But he didn't care. His true objective was to rid Pike County of agitating outsiders, like antipoverty workers, by stoking fears of a communist revolution—and further his own political ambitions.

Al and Margaret McSurely moved to Pike County in April 1967 to help the poor—specifically, poor whites. They'd met about a year before in Washington, DC, where they both did work for the United Planning Organization, or UPO, a War on Poverty community action program. Both were about thirty years old and coming out of failed marriages. They had something else in common: they were committed communists, though neither officially joined the party. And both had worked with black-led civil rights groups—Al with the Congress of Racial Equality (CORE), Margaret with the Student Nonviolent Coordinating Committee (SNCC)—and both had come to believe that, in Margaret's words, "black people should run their own programs, since white people, no matter how well meaning they were, ended up by taking over."

The McSurelys spent a good part of the winter of 1966–67 traveling the country, searching for a place to settle down and begin their lives— and their work—together. "Finally, we chose to move to the Southern mountains and work with poor whites," Margaret recalled in *Freedom Spent*, a book by Richard Harris that examines the sedition case. "We thought the poor people were going to make a revolution."

Pike County was the lion's den for antipoverty workers like the McSurelys. If coal was king in eastern Kentucky, Pike County was the capital of the kingdom. It produced more coal than any other county in the nation. The population of the county seat, Pikeville, was just five thousand, but according to a *Louisville Courier-Journal* survey in the summer of 1967, it counted among its residents some fifty coal millionaires and about forty attorneys. Officials in Pike County were known to be especially hostile to "outside agitators." It's worth noting that Robert Kennedy's eastern Kentucky itinerary originally included a stop in Pikeville, but at the last minute the stop was canceled, allegedly due to time constraints.

Al McSurely went to work for the Appalachian Volunteers, but was "red-baited" out of the organization after a month. A copy of his radical manifesto had circulated among AV managers, who wanted nothing to do with it—or him. So he joined Margaret in working for the Southern Conference Education Fund. Although Ratliff described them as radicals hell-bent on overthrowing the government of Pike County, the McSurelys never really accomplished much in the way of fomenting revolution in eastern Kentucky. They'd only lived there a little more than four months when they were arrested for sedition.

The McSurelys and Mulloy were locked up in the Pike County jail. Mulloy quickly posted a $5,000 bond, but the McSureleys refused to post bond ($5,000 for Al, $2,000 for Margaret) on principle.

They were probably safer in jail anyway. Ratliff's rhetoric had inflamed passions in Pike County. Their attorney, Dan Jack Combs, was receiving death threats. "When this thing broke, there was mass hysteria here," Combs later recalled. "One man told my wife, 'You better tell Dan Jack to pack his bags when we run these Communists out of town. He is one of them. No one else would defend them. We'll shoot him if he doesn't get out.'" Wild rumors began to circulate. According to one, a band of Red Guards from China was coming to Pikeville to break the McSurelys out of jail. Alas, such an invasion proved unnecessary. After a week in jail, the couple finally posted bond and were released.

It was around this time that Steve Cawood became involved with the case. Two of his law school professors had volunteered to assist in the McSurelys' defense. "I can remember going up there [to Pikeville] and clerking for them. All I was doing was carrying books and researching. We stayed at a brand-new motel in Pikeville called the Landmark Inn. It had been built and was owned by Tom Ratliff, who was the prosecuting attorney at the time. And we didn't have enough sense to know at the time that it was his motel."

Were the rooms bugged? "Shit yeah, they were bugged. And we didn't even have enough sense to know or even be concerned about that. Lord have mercy. Later we were told that [the rooms were bugged]. We were paranoid about being in Pikeville because there was such an anticommunist reaction to the whole thing. And the AVs, those kids in Pike County were just red-baited to death over it. I believe those kids all had to move out of Pike County."

As expected, the charges against the McSurelys and Mulloy were eventually thrown out. In September 1967, a three-judge federal panel ruled Kentucky's sedition statute unconstitutional "under even the most flexible yardstick." Bert Combs, a Democratic former governor of Kentucky appointed to the federal bench by Lyndon Johnson, wrote the majority opinion in the two-to-one ruling.

> The statute in question . . . contravenes the First Amendment to the Constitution of the United States because it unduly prohibits freedom of speech, freedom of the press, and the right of assembly. It fails to distinguish between the advocacy of ideas and the advocacy of action. It makes it a criminal offense merely to possess, with intent to circulate, literature on the subject of sedition. It imposes the penalty of imprisonment for advocating an unpopular political belief. It would turn the courts into a forum for argument of political theories with imprisonment the penalty for the loser. It contains no requirement of criminal intent. The unwary and the ignorant could be enmeshed in the dragnet as easily as the covert plotter.

Two months later, in November 1967, Ratliff lost the election for lieutenant governor, but he continued to pursue a lucrative career in mining. When he died at age eighty-eight in April 2015, his obituary noted that he was "a pioneer in [mining techniques such as] the use of roof bolts, scoops, [and] continuous miners, and constructed the first stacking tubes and underground feeders in Pike County."

In December 1967, Margaret McSurely gave birth to a healthy baby boy named Victor. By the time Robert Kennedy visited eastern Kentucky two months later, the sedition case should have been over. The McSurelys had demanded the return of all the material that Ratliff had confiscated from their home. But Ratliff had already forwarded the material to the Senate committee in Washington, which refused to return it.

On February 13, 1968—the same day Kennedy arrived in Kentucky—the McSurelys petitioned the US Supreme Court for the return of their property. "The committee is not searching for information," the petition read. "The committee is trying to destroy those who may have views which vary from the views of the committee."

Incredibly, the case would drag on for another fifteen years—well into the presidency of Ronald Reagan—before the McSurelys finally prevailed.

14

2:30 PM—Barwick

AROUND 2:30 PM, THE KENNEDY CARAVAN arrived at another one-room schoolhouse. Sitting on the banks of a small creek in an isolated community called Barwick, the school, like the one in Vortex, had seen better days. There was no indoor plumbing—the students used outhouses, one up the hill for the boys, one down by the creek for the girls—and the obligatory potbellied stove sat squatly in the middle of the room. The thirty or so students in grades one through eight sat at battered wooden desks. Their teacher, Bonnie Jean Carroll, thirty-three at the time, had attended this very same school as a child herself, and may well have sat at one of the desks her pupils now occupied.

Even his most bitter political opponents could not deny that Robert Kennedy's affection for children was deep and often moving. He was the father of ten and utterly comfortable around children. He had an almost telepathic connection with them, and they seemed to sense it.

"In many ways he'd rather talk to kids than grown-ups," Peter Edelman tells me. "His connection with kids was genuine. He'd pick up a kid in a motorcade and start talking to him and they'd get all the way across town and he'd still have the kid with him."

On Christmas Eve 1963, in his first public appearance after his brother's assassination, Kennedy visited an orphanage in Washington. The author and journalist Peter Maas remembered the event.

A little boy—I don't suppose he was more than six or seven years old—suddenly darted forward, and stopped in front of him, and said, "Your brother's dead! Your brother's dead!" Gosh, you know, you could hear a pin drop. The adults, all of us, we just kind of turned away. . . . The little boy knew he had done something wrong, but he didn't know *what*; so he started to cry. Bobby stepped forward and picked him up, in kind of one motion, and held him very close for a moment, and he said, "That's all right. I have another brother."

He had the same effect on the children at the Barwick school. As he moved from desk to desk, Kennedy was crowded by newspaper photographers, as well as cameramen filming the event for the evening news. But Kennedy's gentle manner put the children at ease. He smiled and crouched down close to them and spoke softly. Sometimes he held their hands. He looked through their textbooks and asked them what they'd had for breakfast. Most had had cold cereal; a few said they'd had no breakfast at all. The children were, understandably, somewhat intimidated by this important stranger and the imposing entourage that accompanied him.

"We wound up, with some difficulty, at a remote one-room schoolhouse," William Greider, who covered the trip for the *Louisville Courier-Journal*, recalled years later in a letter to the playwright John Malpede.

The caravan dropped down into a mountain cove, causing great excitement. Kennedy led the way into the schoolroom, followed by the herd of reporters and cameras. Inside, the children were something like terrified, frozen to their little school desks, too nervous even to look at the great man directly.

Kennedy grasped the grotesque quality of the moment. He had come to cheer them up, offer words of hope. They were in deep culture shock.

So the senator made no remarks. He shook hands maybe with the teacher, but then moved wordlessly among the rows of desks, pausing beside a child here and there, stooping down and taking the child's hand, sometimes murmuring a few words that none of us could hear. It was a powerful moment, this famous man communicating to these scared children with his physical humanity alone.

He did that for a time, then departed. The caravan rumbled off.

Kennedy believed that education was fundamental to ending poverty, and what he saw in eastern Kentucky alarmed him: dilapidated facilities, poor transportation, politicized school administrations, underpaid and overworked teachers. The median years of schooling in Breathitt County was about seven and a half, and functional illiteracy (four years of schooling or less) ranged from 23 to 30 percent of the adult population (the national average was 7.8 percent).

But what appalled him most was the chronic underfunding of the region's schools, despite its vast mineral wealth. Coal companies paid no severance taxes—that is, no taxes on the coal they mined (or "severed" from the earth). They paid only property taxes on the assessed value of the land and equipment they owned, and even these taxes were artificially deflated, because the companies controlled the county officials who determined tax rates and assessments. Mining equipment—but not food, clothing, and medicine—was exempted from the 3 percent state sales tax.

So, in Pike County, for example, $65 million worth of coal was mined in 1966, but local taxes covered only 18.3 percent of the county's $4.1 million school budget—the state had to make up the difference—and 45 percent of the population lived below the poverty line.

In Kennedy's opinion, it was nothing short of criminal. While corporations like Bethlehem Steel—number seventeen on the 1967 Fortune 500—got rich off Kentucky coal, children in eastern Kentucky were required to purchase their own textbooks every year, at a cost of as much as thirty-five dollars. Children whose families could not afford to purchase the books simply made do without them.

"I think of the great wealth that exists in eastern Kentucky," Kennedy would say later that day. "It seems to me that some of that wealth should be utilized in-state and remain here. So that you can pay the teachers' salaries. You think of all the wealth that's been taken out of eastern Kentucky over the last forty or fifty years, it's astronomical. And yet schools haven't been constructed and teachers aren't being paid adequate salaries. There are not the roads and the highways there should be. And there's not the industry there should be. Somebody's taking the money."

15

Three Licks and a Smile

IN THE SUMMER OF 2018, I met up with Bonnie Jean Carroll at her church, Coneva Church of God, in Chavies, a small town just three miles from the one-room schoolhouse she taught at in Barwick. Now eighty-three and slightly hunched, with big glasses that give her an owlish aspect, Bonnie Carroll is a tiny woman who has made a big impact on many lives. "I've tried to be a great asset to my community," she tells me, "and that makes you feel good."

Born in Breathitt County in 1935, she was the second of twelve children. Her father was a coal miner, her mother a homemaker. She was raised by an aunt and uncle. "There was love in our family," she says, "but Mom and Dad married at a very early age and started having babies." After attending the Barwick school, she went to Breathitt High School in the county seat of Jackson, about thirty miles away. "I had to walk two miles to catch a train to Breathitt High every day," she tells me. "I didn't mind. You can like it or not like it, so you may as well like it."

She started teaching straight out of high school. Her starting salary was about $140 a month. She later earned a bachelor's degree from Eastern Kentucky State College through a distance-learning program. In 1973 she went to work for the county's Head Start program, and she stayed there until she retired—in 2017, when she was eighty-two.

"I'll tell you what, when I had to quit, I wasn't satisfied. I'd rather be teaching now if I was able. I loved teaching. That was my life. My kids

Bonnie Jean Carroll, photographed at Coneva Church of God in Chavies, Kentucky, February 2019. *Lou Murrey*

was my life." She's lost count of how many children she taught over the years—hundreds, for sure. "I was in Lexington and this boy said to me, 'How are you?' and I said, 'Fine,' and he said, 'You were my teacher.' And that happens often. They tap me on the shoulder and I turn around and it's someone six foot and it's one of my kids!"

Teaching in a one-room schoolhouse may sound quaint, like something out of *Little House on the Prairie*, but it was exhausting work. The teacher was responsible for cleaning and maintaining the building, ordering the coal and stoking the fire, and, of course, preparing lesson plans for multiple grades. Like most teachers in one-room schools, Bonnie says she got a lot of help from her older students. "I was fortunate, I had a boy or two that would build my fire and see that everything was OK when we went home," she tells me. "And the older girls would help with the younger kids, reading stories to them. They did quite a bit of help."

Since most of her students were very poor, Bonnie was sometimes responsible for their material needs as well. She made sure they had decent clothes and even fed them from time to time. She was

A typical one-room school in eastern Kentucky, circa 1967. *Berea College Special Collections and Archives, Berea, Kentucky*

especially adamant that they have reading material. "Many of them came from homes with no magazines, no newspapers, no books at home."

"Kids would come to you for anything," she says. "I was more like a social worker than a teacher."

She says she's not sure why her school was chosen to be the one Kennedy visited. (Peter Edelman can't recall either.) A few VISTA volunteers had worked at the school, so maybe they put it on Kennedy's radar. Bonnie's theory: "I think he wanted to go to the poorest school—one of the poorest—and that was us." She says she had only a day's notice before the visit—not that she needed to do much to prepare. "I always kept a clean classroom," she says.

"It was interesting," she says of Kennedy's visit. "I always liked the Kennedys very much. I really believe he [Robert Kennedy] cared about the poor. He was really a friendly person."

"I'd give the world for a Kennedy man today," she adds. "To me—I might be wrong—we're supposed to be as good as our word, and I believe they were, the Kennedys."

She doesn't think much of modern politicians. "Oh my goodness, sometimes I turn that TV off and say I'm not turning it back on anymore. I think we need a lot more politicians with courage." As for Donald Trump? "Sometimes I like him, sometimes I don't," says Bonnie, a lifelong Democrat. "I wouldn't want anything to happen to him, but he's odd. Let's say that. He's an odd person. And I get angry with him sometimes."

"I just hope and pray it gets better before it gets worse," she says, finally.

In late December 2018, I returned to Bonnie Carroll's church to meet with her again. This time she brought along two of her students from the 1967–68 school year: her son, Billy Dean Carroll, who was ten at the time, and Taylor Smith, who was eleven. Remarkably, Billy was absent the day Kennedy visited, though neither he nor his mother remembers why. They assume he must have been sick—very sick—for him to miss such a special occasion. But Taylor was there and remembers the day well. "He shook my hand," he says. "Asked us how we was."

Taylor says attending a one-room school had its benefits. "I used to listen to Bonnie teaching the next grade up. I thought, *If I hurry up and finish my assignment, I can listen.* Helped me get ahead a little bit." He had some trouble adjusting to high school, however. "You go from a one-room school to a school where you have to change classes. I was lost!"

Bonnie had brought along a photo of the student body, an underexposed snapshot of twenty-eight smiling students standing in front of a blackboard draped with garland—the photo was taken around Christmas. Billy and Taylor studied it closely, scanning the faces of their long-ago schoolmates. Memories came flooding back, as they must. In a way, this group of youngsters embodied Robert Kennedy's hopes and fears for Appalachia.

Billy and Taylor concluded that most of their schoolmates left Breathitt County after school—but that most of those who left have since

Billy Dean Carroll (left) and Taylor Smith look over old class photos from the Barwick school, December 2018. *Author's photo*

returned. Only four of the twenty-eight are deceased: two by natural causes and two by suicide. "The ones that are still going," says Taylor, "are doing good, really." Billy points at the picture and says, "Not a single one of them was a freeloader, or sorry." ("Sorry" is an eastern Kentucky euphemism for lazy.)

In the years after Kennedy's visit, the schools in eastern Kentucky improved. In 1972 the Kentucky legislature finally imposed a severance tax on coal: a minimum of thirty cents per ton. This generated millions of dollars in new revenue that was sent back to the counties for roads and schools. "They built roads to the head of these hollers and everywhere else," Billy explains. "And that about done it for the one-room schools. Once they had the roads in, you could easily transport" students to bigger schools. The Barwick school closed around 1972.

In 1965 there were 553 one-room schools in Kentucky. By 1975 there were just nine, all in the eastern mountains. In 1989 the last one-room school, Lower Leatherwood Elementary in Perry County, closed.

The one-room schoolhouse that Kennedy visited in Barwick, Kentucky, in February 1968, photographed February 2019. *Lou Murrey*

Of Robert Kennedy, Billy Dean Carroll says there's no doubt in his mind that he would've been elected president if he'd lived. "He would've been to the white people of Appalachia—the poor—he would've been like Martin Luther King was to the blacks. A lot of things happened just because he drove into this area and got out and talked to people. Things did develop from that. It excited the politicians and leaders at that time. Everybody had that feeling. You just had a certain feeling, even at the age I was. If he'd become president this place would be totally different than what you see it now. There's no industry here. The coal industry is it. And it's basically died. They holler, 'It's coming back.' It may come back for a few years, but politics is gonna change. I am for the environment. But I am for coal. I'm for jobs. But I am for not destroying the environment. So I'm a Demo-pub, I guess! A Democrat-Republican. But anyway, there's no industry here."

Taylor adds, "This place did start moving after he was here. We got recognized more, just because Robert Kennedy come to this part of the country." As for his grade school teacher, Taylor has nothing but kind words. "She was the best, Bonnie was. Now I'm telling you, she was a fine teacher."

"Everybody loved Bonnie," Billy agrees. "When she used the paddle, it was three licks and a smile."

After the Barwick school closed, the building was converted into a library, but by the early 1980s it had been abandoned. Remarkably, the building is still standing. I ask Bonnie if she wants to ride along when I drive out to see it, but she declines. The last time she drove by the old school, she tells me, "I could've cried. I was so hurt. It was beautiful at one time. Vandals just destroyed it. It was a mess."

Indeed it was. Its white paint peeling and its windows broken, the once-fine wood-frame building where generations of mountain children learned their ABCs, and where a famous senator once stopped to learn something himself, today stands forlorn, slowly collapsing in on itself. Dense vegetation has grown up around the building. I want to go inside, to see if the potbellied stove and the chalkboard are still in there, but a friendly neighbor warns me against such an adventure. "I wouldn't go in there," he says. "Them weeds is real snakey." I heed his advice.

16

3:30 PM—Hazard

FROM BARWICK, KENNEDY TRAVELED twenty miles southeast to Hazard, a town of fifty-five hundred and the seat of Perry County. Both the town and the county are named for Oliver Hazard Perry, a War of 1812 naval hero who commanded a force of one hundred Kentucky volunteers hastily recruited for sea duty from General William Henry Harrison's land forces. Most of the Kentuckians had never seen a ship before, but in the September 1813 Battle of Lake Erie, "dressed in their favorite linsey-woolsey hunting shirts and drawers" and perched high in the rigging of the American vessels, they used their famous long rifles to torment the British fleet and help win the battle.

Hazard, Kentucky, is not to be confused with the fictional Hazzard County, Georgia, the home of television's *Dukes of Hazzard*, though the nonfictional Hazard was happy to fill in for the fake one in 1981, when several stars of the show served as grand marshals of the town's annual Black Gold Festival parade. The Duke boys couldn't make it, but Sheriff Rosco P. Coltrane, Daisy Duke, and Boss Hogg attended, making the event the biggest thing that had happened in Hazard since Robert Kennedy came to town thirteen years earlier.

On the day Kennedy visited, the *Hazard Herald* carried a front-page editorial welcoming the senator to town but also warning him that the solution to Appalachia's problems was not a "government hand-out."

Appalachia is a land of "proud people." Even those who have few in material possessions, are extremely proud of their religious and cultural beliefs. We worked hard and live clean, spirited lives.

We welcome you, Senator Kennedy, and your entire group to Eastern Kentucky, and we pray that you will understand that while we are poor in some ways, we are rich in many others. All we ask for is a chance to better ourselves through a government which is said to be "of the people, by the people and for the people."

Accompanied by Hazard mayor Willie Dawahare, Kennedy toured Liberty Street, the town's small African American neighborhood, where the streets were unpaved and the houses in disrepair. Dawahare, the son of Syrian immigrants and owner of a chain of clothing stores, explained to Kennedy that Hazard had applied for federal loans to redevelop Liberty Street, but the Department of Housing and Urban Development was dragging its feet approving them. "I mean . . . they're so slow," Dawahare complained. "I don't know what's going to happen now."

Kennedy told Dawahare he'd see what he could do. Within months the loans were approved. Liberty Street was finally paved, and new public housing was constructed. The redevelopment of Liberty Street was often cited to me as one of the War on Poverty's crowning achievements in Perry County.

As he toured Liberty Street, Kennedy was, as usual, trailed by a large group of people. While most politicians worry about drawing a crowd, Kennedy worried about getting trampled by one. Among the two to three hundred people surrounding Kennedy was Dee Davis, a sixteen-year-old Hazard High School student curious to see the famous senator for himself. Although he considered himself a Republican, Davis rushed home that afternoon and brushed his hair so it flipped across his forehead just like Kennedy's before heading out to join the throngs on Liberty Street. His ancestors were some of the first white settlers in Kentucky, and Davis grew up in relatively comfortable circumstances. His father owned a furniture store in town, and the family was "definitely" middle class, he says, though he adds, paraphrasing Mark Twain, "We were neither poor nor conspicuously scrupulous."

Kennedy touring the Liberty Street neighborhood in Hazard, Kentucky, February 13, 1968. *Berea College Special Collections and Archives, Berea, Kentucky*

On Liberty Street, Kennedy visited the home of George Olinger, where he found "a horde of children watching an afternoon quiz show on the TV." When he asked them what they'd had for breakfast that morning, they answered: "Nothing." All the while, their father dozed in an easy chair, seemingly oblivious to the famous visitor in his home.

Kennedy's visit was meant to open the rest of the nation's eyes to the problem of poverty in Appalachia, but it also opened many Appalachians' eyes to the dire conditions in which their neighbors lived. Dee Davis was good friends with the Olinger children—they played ball together, he tells me—and when Kennedy stepped into their home, Davis had what he calls a "moment of awareness": "I was looking through the front window, looking at those kids and the reporters with their notebooks, and I thought, *OK, I guess they're poor, and now the whole country is going to see that they're poor. And they [the reporters] are defining us by how we're different from other Americans.* It wasn't a black-white issue. It was a poverty issue."

Today, Dee Davis is the director of the Center for Rural Strategies in Whitesburg, about thirty miles east of Hazard. The organization promotes economic and cultural development in rural communities. As he prepares breakfast—scrambled eggs with a pickle on the side—for me and his wife in the kitchen of their home on a hill overlooking downtown Whitesburg, Davis says too many Appalachians no longer appreciate just how hard life was for many people before the War on Poverty. "Poor schoolkids used lard for hair gel," he says. "I have a buddy who says he dropped out because in the wintertime the lard would solidify on the walk to school and everybody could see it."

"It's a big change when someone goes from privation and danger to safety and opportunity," he adds. The challenge now, Davis says, is to capitalize on those changes. "People are not just going to do each other's nails and walk each other's dogs. There needs to be a lot more than that."

17

5:00 PM—Yellow Creek, a Guy Who Wore Horns

KENNEDY WANTED TO VISIT A STRIP MINE, SO on the way from Hazard to Alice Lloyd College in Pippa Passes, the caravan stopped at one on a hillside above Yellow Creek, just outside Vicco, an old coal town in Perry County named for the Virginia Iron, Coal and Coke Company.

The Yellow Creek operation was owned by William Bartram Sturgill, one of the most powerful and feared mine operators in eastern Kentucky. Born in Floyd County in 1924, Bill Sturgill was a star athlete at the University of Kentucky, where he played basketball for the legendary coach Adolph Rupp. He was expected to go into politics—his father was twice elected Floyd County sheriff—but after he graduated, Bill went into the mining business instead and became a strip mining pioneer in eastern Kentucky. He was probably the first strip mine millionaire in the United States, if not the world.

In 1959 Sturgill and his partner Dick Kelly founded Kentucky Oak Mining Company. In 1961 the company was awarded a multiyear contract to provide the Tennessee Valley Authority seventy-five hundred tons of coal a week—nearly four hundred thousand tons a year. Under pressure to fulfill the TVA contract, Kentucky Oak began leasing mineral rights and strip mining wherever it could. Nearly all the land the company mined was under broad-form deeds. Kentucky Oak also began experimenting with new strip mining techniques. The company ordered the largest auger ever built to that time, a seven-foot-wide drill bit nicknamed the Kelly Giant (after Sturgill's business partner). The Kelly Giant could penetrate eight hundred feet into a coal seam and extract more than four hundred tons of coal an hour.

"Operating on a tight profit margin," wrote Chad Montrie in *To Save the Land and People*, a history of strip mining in Appalachia, "the strip mining pair [Sturgill and Kelly] neglected to gain the permission of landowners to extract coal under their property, which they did not need in any case, and they did little to repair the damage left in their wake." By the mid-1960s, Sturgill and his company were facing a raft of lawsuits—not to mention threats of violence—from furious landowners. It was one of Sturgill's bulldozers that the widow Ollie Combs sat in front of in November 1965. "Although local people protested the noise, the blasting, the landslides and the flooding caused by denuding of the steep slopes, and the ruining of their roads by overloaded coal trucks, their protests were to no avail," wrote Harry Caudill, author of *Night Comes to the Cumberlands*. "The governors heard the complaints but heeded Sturgill, who characterized the critics as 'emotional' and the floods as 'acts of God.'" ("If he thought he couldn't get in the papers," Sturgill once said of Caudill, "he'd never open his mouth.")

In an oral history interview recorded in 1988 for the Louie B. Nunn Center for Oral History at the University of Kentucky, Sturgill admitted, "We were doing things wrong" in the early 1960s. "We did everything by trial and error."

In 1970 Sturgill and Kelly sold Kentucky Oak Mining Company to Falcon Seaboard, a Houston-based energy company, for a reported $10.5 million (about $66 million in today's dollars). After that, Sturgill still dabbled in mining but mostly pursued his civic and philanthropic interests. In the 1980s he served as the secretary of Kentucky's combined agriculture and energy departments, and as the chairman of the Kentucky State Racing Commission. He also served eighteen years on the University of Kentucky board of trustees, including ten years as chairman. He died in July 2014, just shy of his ninetieth birthday.

"I would like for people to remember that I was a useful citizen and established my time in supporting the priorities of Kentucky: education and roads and social services and health care," Sturgill said in that oral history interview. "That's what I would like to be remembered as, rather than a guy who wore horns and [*chuckle*] did all those ugly things, because I have a very sensitive feeling about that."

18

Hell, I'll Handle This

IT WAS PROBABLY NO ACCIDENT that Kennedy chose to visit a Sturgill mine. If he was going to take on the strip mining industry, he might as well take on the biggest and baddest strip miner of them all. "We weren't supposed to go up there," Steve Cawood recalls. "Nobody was supposed to go up there. Perkins didn't want to. Perkins's style wasn't confrontational. Bill Sturgill was an institution at the time.

"I was in the car with Perkins, Bobby, and the state trooper who was driving. Maybe Peter [Edelman] was in the car. We drove up the road to the gate of the mine. Bill Sturgill employed a guy who was in the guard shack. The superintendent was down at the gate; they had somehow gotten word that Bobby was planning to visit.

"The trooper got out at the gate and talked to the superintendent and came back and said, 'We can't go up there.' And there was a guard at the shack who was armed. And Bobby jumped out and I thought the trooper was gonna drop his drawers. And Bobby jumped out and said, 'Hell, I'll handle this.'

"Bobby was giving orders, let me just put it that way. Bobby was not bothered at all, but the rest of us were just nervous as hell. I mean, Sturgill's people had a reputation, they'd whip protesters trying to stop the equipment and push people around—just real bullies—and we didn't know what was gonna happen. But Bobby was just courageous as hell about it. And he went out there mouthing around with Bill's superintendent. He wasn't being a horse's ass, but he was being stern, because that's what his job was. And Bobby basically said, 'We're going up there.' He climbed back into the car and said, 'Let's go.' And the people parted and we drove up."

Yellow Creek was an excellent example of contour (or bench) mining, a method of strip mining that requires miners to carve an L-shaped "bench" out of the side of a mountain to expose a coal seam. The "overburden" is dumped down the mountain, creating what is known as a spoil pile. The exposed vertical surface—the back of the bench—is known as the highwall. The flat horizontal surface serves as the road for equipment to access the coal in the highwall. Sometimes the bench will wrap around the mountain. At intervals it is connected to access roads, like the one that Kennedy's Chrysler Imperial ascended on that winter day in 1968.*

By now Harry Caudill had joined the caravan, as had Milton Ogle, the director of the Appalachian Volunteers, the OEO-funded group that had recently started organizing protests against strip mining. It would have been harder to find two men in eastern Kentucky whom Sturgill loathed more at that moment than Caudill and Ogle. Except maybe Bobby Kennedy. It was probably a good thing Sturgill wasn't there. He'd assigned one of his lieutenants, a mine foreman named Roy Mullins, to deal with the uninvited guests.

Mullins was waiting for the caravan when it reached the bench. He told Kennedy he was "more than welcome" to inspect the strip mine, "so long as the inspection is objective." But Mullins said Kennedy could not tour the mine without a guide. "There are men working up ahead and a lot of equipment," he said. "We don't want any injuries or damage." And the "pleasure seekers"—Caudill and Ogle—were not welcome. They would have to stay behind while Kennedy was shown around.

The senator objected to Mullins's conditions. He wanted to tour the site unescorted, and with whomever he chose. By now the rest of the

---

* Imperfect record keeping and fading memories have made it difficult to find the exact location of the Yellow Creek strip mine today. I asked a few people I met in and around Vicco if they knew where it was. None did. Steve Cawood doesn't remember. Even the Kentucky Division of Mine Reclamation and Enforcement isn't sure.

Mine foreman Roy Mullins (left), Robert Kennedy (center), and Congress-man Carl Perkins (right) at the Yellow Creek strip mine near Vicco, Kentucky, February 13, 1968. *Berea College Special Collections and Archives, Berea, Kentucky*

caravan had reached the bench, and reporters surrounded Mullins and the Kennedy entourage. The atmosphere was tense. According to the *Washington Post*'s Richard Harwood, "All over the mountain, carloads of hard-eyed guards blocked off roadways to places Sturgill had declared off limits," and there were "rumors of gunplay and trespassing."

"We didn't know if we were gonna get shot going up there or what," Steve Cawood recalls. "The paranoia was brutal. They were operating. There's heavy equipment running around, and the coal trucks taking the coal down from the mountain to the tipple were running past us, creating big clouds of dust. Bobby wanted to talk to the mine employ-ees. He wanted to ask them how they felt about it. I can hear Perkins telling him, 'Now Bobby, they just work here. They're just earning a damn living.' Perkins was just such a lovable character. Nobody else in the car could say that: 'Now Bobby.' Like he's speaking to his child, y'know."

Kennedy at the Yellow Creek strip mine. Behind him on the left is Milton Ogle, the director of the Appalachian Volunteers. *Berea College Special Collections and Archives, Berea, Kentucky*

Even without touring the site, Cawood says, Kennedy could plainly see the operation and the mine's devastating impact on the environment. "I'd never been on a strip job where you could see in 360 degrees utter destruction from strip mining. If we'd tried we couldn't have found a better location to take him to. He was just shocked. He was just shocked."

It called to mind Harry Caudill's description in *Night Comes to the Cumberlands*: "Decay spreads across a land ruined by the abrasion of deluge."

It was cold and getting dark. Kennedy was running late for his next event at Alice Lloyd College, twenty miles away in Pippa Passes. Mullins kept stalling and ran out the clock. Kennedy rode back down the mountain in Mullins's car.

"We are a legitimate industry," Mullins told Kennedy when they reached the gate. "We believe in reclamation. All we ask is that the people who come in here look objectively."

As he left, Kennedy sarcastically thanked Mullins for "the objective tour I just received."

The caravan of reporters' cars that followed Kennedy, parked at the Yellow Creek strip mine. *Berea College Special Collections and Archives, Berea, Kentucky*

"I just couldn't see the purpose of his visit," Mullins told a reporter after Kennedy left. "We have enough trouble in Appalachia already without him criticizing an industry that paid over $6 million in salaries last year."

KENNEDY IS BLOCKED ON STRIP MINE TOUR, read the headline above a small story about the contretemps in the next day's *New York Times*. Admittedly, the story was buried on page 56, beneath a review of George Balanchine's performance as the titular character in the ballet *Don Quixote* at the New York State Theater.

The big news in the paper that day was the Pentagon's announcement that an extra 10,500 troops were being rushed to Vietnam for "insurance purposes," pushing the total number of US troops in the country over the half-million mark for the first time. (The number would peak at 543,482 on April 30, 1968.)

Kennedy chatting with reporters at the Yellow Creek strip mine.
Berea College Special Collections and Archives, Berea, Kentucky

In Memphis, meanwhile, the city's one thousand African American sanitation workers were in the third day of a strike that would roil the nation. On April 4, while in Memphis to lend his support to the striking workers, Martin Luther King Jr. would be assassinated.

In Kentucky, the newly inaugurated Republican governor, Louie Nunn, unveiled his two-year, $2.5 billion state budget proposal to a joint session of the state legislature on the evening of February 13. Nunn, who'd run on a "No New Taxes" platform, proposed a whopping 67 percent increase in the state sales tax, from 3 percent to 5 percent. "I stated, as did others, that I could operate this government within existing revenue," Nunn professed. "But since then, it has been revealed that the financial resources (the estimated revenues plus surplus) would be $24 million less than originally anticipated." In fact, Nunn said, the state's financial condition was so dire that, without an immediate increase in revenue, "I shall have no alternative but to suspend . . . the

Medicaid program, old age benefits, public assistance, educational programs and perhaps other public services." Nunn promised that roughly two-thirds of the additional revenue generated by the proposed budget would go to education: "We must move ahead to keep from falling still further behind." The Democratic-controlled legislature would approve the budget overwhelmingly.

19

A Prairie in the Mountains

"I'M ONE OF THE LEAST politically correct wildlife biologists you'll ever meet," David Ledford tells me as we bounce along a deeply rutted and muddy road in his F-150. "I love Roundup." He is showing me around Bailey Hill, a mountain in Bell County, about seven miles east of Pineville.

At least it used to be a mountain. In the late 1970s, a Birmingham, Alabama, construction magnate named John Murdoch Harbert III bought Bailey Hill, lopped off the top, and scooped out the coal inside, kind of like eating a soft-boiled egg. It was one of the first large-scale examples of the strip mining technique known, straightforwardly, as mountaintop removal, or MTR. After the coal was extracted, the hole was filled with rock and dirt. But most of the mountaintop was just blasted into pieces and dumped into the valley below. It's estimated that MTR mining has resulted in the burial of nearly two thousand miles of streams in Appalachia.

So now Bailey Hill looks like a capital A with everything above the crossbar missing. The "mountaintop" is not a peak but a grassy flatland—which David Ledford wants to turn into a nature reserve.

Ledford is big and stocky, with an iron handshake despite the fact his right hand is missing the middle three fingers, the result of a meat grinder accident when he was eighteen ("I didn't even know it had a safety guard," he tells me), and he bears a passing resemblance to the actor John Goodman. Much like his opinion of herbicides, his career path is not common for a wildlife biologist. "I grew up fishing and hunting in eastern Tennessee. Went to college right out of high school. Didn't finish. Went to work for my dad. He owned a gas station. Got married, had two kids. My oldest son was in kindergarten or first grade when a light went on in my head and I said, *I gotta do something else*. So I thought about going back to college, to UT [the University of Tennessee]. I heard you could get a degree in wildlife biology and management and I thought, *That sounds cool*. Drove over and got a list of the classes you have to take, and they sounded pretty neat. Sat down with a wildlife professor, and in twenty minutes I thought, *This is it, I gotta do this*. I didn't even know what a wildlife biologist did."

After college he went to work as a corporate biologist for Stone Container Corporation, a major pulp and paper company. In 2010 he moved to London, Kentucky, and started a nonprofit called the Appalachian Wildlife Foundation. With more than $38 million in public and private funding, the AWF has purchased or leased twelve thousand acres on and around Bailey Hill with hopes of turning the old mine into a world-class wildlife center.

Since Robert Kennedy visited eastern Kentucky in 1968, more than twenty-three hundred square miles—nearly 1.5 million acres—have been stripped in central Appalachia, an area larger than the state of Delaware. And the area keeps expanding. In a 2018 article in the online science journal *PLOS ONE*, researchers reported that, before 1998, about ten square meters of stripped land were required to produce a metric ton of coal. By 2015 it took about thirty square meters—three times as much land—to produce the same amount of coal.*

The fight to stop strip mining has been lost. Ledford says the question now is: What do we do with all that stripped land? "We can sit around and freak out and have a drum circle and braid each other's ponytails and really wish it wouldn't've happened," he says. "But it's happening. We're still gonna use coal. We need coal. That's just reality.

* Generally speaking, mountaintop removal and strip mining (as well as open pit mining) are considered forms of surface mining. That is, all strip mining is surface mining, but not all surface mining is strip mining.

When somebody invents cold fusion, it all goes away and we're good. But until then, this is what we have to work with."

Before the federal Surface Mining Control and Reclamation Act— SMCRA, pronounced, regrettably, "smackra"—was passed in 1977, mine operators weren't required to do much to repair the sites they stripped. State reclamation laws were weak and poorly enforced. Some operators made token efforts. As early as 1964, Bill Sturgill's company, Kentucky Oak Mining Company, began planting apple and peach trees on their abandoned strip mines. "If things go well," Sturgill's business partner Dick Kelly gushed, "the fruit business 15 years from now will be more profitable than the coal business." Bethlehem Steel planted blackberry bushes on some of its land after stripping it, and Bethlehem executives were fond of handing out jars of "reclaimed" blackberry jam, allegedly made by church groups. ("Smackra" would've been a good name for the jam!)

In 1972 the Kentucky Surface Mining and Reclamation Association, a group funded by Bethlehem and other mining companies, launched a public relations campaign with the cumbersome tagline, "Kentucky: The Proud Land. First in Coal Production. First in Land Reclamation." In full-page newspaper ads and a thirty-minute film, the group touted reclamation "success stories": homes and a community center built—and cattle grazing contentedly—on reclaimed land. But these were Potemkin villages. A subsequent investigation published in the alternative journalism review *(MORE)*—yes, the parentheses were part of the name; it was that kind of magazine—found the images had been carefully staged: "They show the best reclamation projects, photographed at angles that hide the bare highways left by the strippers."

Even the regulations imposed by SMCRA, supposedly a tough law, are less than stringent. A mine operator is required to restore a stripped site to its "approximate original contour," so that it "closely resembles the general surface configuration of the land prior to mining." But the phrase "approximate original contour" was never defined, a gaping loophole that you could drive a bucket-wheel excavator through (albeit very slowly). SMCRA also requires mine operators to minimize erosion by revegetating a site after it's been stripped. This often entails spraying the site with a mixture of seed, fertilizer, lime, mulch, and water, a process known as hydroseeding.

Unfortunately, for many years the most commonly used seed was sericea lespedeza, a plant that was introduced in the United States from Japan in the 1890s. Sericea lespedeza—spoken out loud, its name is almost lyrical: suh-REE-zuh less-puh-DEE-zuh—grows fast and thick, with deep roots, which is great for arresting erosion but terrible for native plants, which are quickly choked out. David Ledford calls it "sericea crap," and it's what was used to revegetate the stump of Bailey Hill. "It's great at stabilizing soil," he says. "It was going to be the miracle plant for cattle farming. For hay, for grazing. This was going to be a boom for the cattle industry. It was planted in a lot of places. And now most everybody wishes it had never been brought to the United States."

When we reach the plateau at the top of the stunted mountain, Ledford puts his pickup in park and we get out for a look around. The landscape is disconcerting. We're standing on a grassy plain dotted with giant spools of hay—local farmers harvest it—but in the distance on all sides stand densely wooded mountains shrouded in low clouds. It's like a piece of Kansas has been plopped down in the middle of the Appalachian Mountains.

Ledford's plan is to kill off all the sericea lespedeza with controlled burns and herbicides. Then the native plants will reclaim the land: goldenrod, ragweed, Queen Anne's lace, milkweed. What was once a wooded mountain—then a mountaintop removal mine—will become a prairie grassland. If all goes well, the new plants will attract dozens of species

The plateau at the top of Bailey Hill, on the site of a mountaintop removal mine. *Author's photo*

of birds—bobwhite quail, grasshopper sparrow—as well as butterflies and other insects. "Monarch butterflies need milkweed to reproduce," Ledford explains. "Well, monarch butterflies are in big trouble—major trouble. One of the reasons is big monoculture agriculture. When you're growing soybeans and corn, you don't have milkweed. It's not there, where it used to be, out in the prairie. Well, on these big mines you get milkweed."

"Bobwhite quail are an imperiled grassland species that's in trouble because our grassland habitats are gone," Ledford says. "Across this country. They're just gone. But you can find them on these old mines."

We're back in the pickup now, driving back down the mountain. Suddenly Ledford stops and kills the engine. "Hear that?" he asks. There's a quiet chirping in the distance. "That's a grasshopper sparrow," he says. "They're in big trouble. They live in prairies. Where the prairies used to be are now horse farms, subdivisions, soybeans, and corn. The prairies are gone. These mines provide this grassland habitat, and it's big enough that they can actually get on these mine sites and thrive." So the ugly flat mountains of eastern Kentucky could help save species displaced by the bucolic horse farms of western Kentucky. "Nobody complains about horse farms," says Ledford as he starts the pickup back up, "but that's where the prairies used to be in this state!"

Ledford also plans to import several hundred head of elk. The Appalachian Wildlife Center is scheduled to open in 2021.* "This will be a tourist attraction," Ledford says. "We've had to do numerous feasibility studies, and this is gonna be a big deal. In our fourth or fifth year, we're gonna hit the 850,000 paid visitor mark. When you bring 850,000 people in one year to this spot on the planet, they will spend $167 million in a six-county, seven-county area. When you do that over a period of five years, the ripple effect leads to the creation of about twenty-eight hundred jobs. So it's creating a whole new economic force, a whole new economic paradigm of outdoor recreation, wildlife recreation."

Ledford says the wildlife center will attract bird watchers, elk enthusiasts, and wildlife fans in general. (Hunting will be prohibited.) He predicts many of the tourists will stop by on their way to attractions

---

* In October 2019 the Appalachian Wildlife Center's name was changed to Boone's Ridge.

farther south in Tennessee: Dollywood, Gatlinburg, Great Smoky Mountains National Park. "We need a very small percentage of those people to come here to hit our numbers," he says.

The Appalachian Wildlife Center is just the latest in a long line of proposed uses for abandoned strip mines, economic development projects meant to supplement—or replace—coal mining jobs. The wildlife center's visitors center will be built on the site of an unfinished industrial park—industrial parks being a favorite reclamation project for abandoned strip mines; eastern Kentucky is dotted with them, many of which are either completely or partially vacant. Other popular uses for abandoned strip mines include ATV trails, golf courses, prisons, airports, baseball diamonds, "scenic pastureland," public parks, and housing developments.

Reclaiming abandoned mines isn't easy; many of the sites are polluted by heavy metals created by the mining process, as well as a toxic goo known as coal sludge or slurry. As a result, a 2010 Associated Press investigation found, "Of the more than 345,700 acres of mining lands in eastern Kentucky that have been approved for a specific post-mining purpose, just over 6,300 acres, or about 1.8 percent, have been designated for 'commercial,' 'industrial,' or 'residential' developments." And a 2009 survey by the Natural Resources Defense Council found that almost 90 percent of 410 reclaimed mountaintop removal sites surveyed "had no form of verifiable post-mining economic reclamation excluding forestry and pasture."

Strip mining's proponents have long claimed reclaimed sites would revitalize Appalachia—Kentucky Republican senator Rand Paul has said strip mining "enhances" the land, and West Virginia Democratic senator Joe Manchin calls reclamation a "principal tool" of economic development—but the results, after more than fifty years, are negligible. Remember Dick Kelly's 1964 prediction that fruit would be more profitable than coal in fifteen years? He was wrong.

20

The *Globe* Woman

WHEN BOSTON'S FENWAY PARK OPENED ON APRIL 20, 1912, Robert Kennedy's maternal grandfather, Boston mayor John "Honey Fitz" Fitzgerald, threw out the ceremonial first pitch. Less than six months later, on October 10, the mayor returned to Fenway to watch game 3 of the 1912 World Series, with his beloved Red Sox taking on the hated New York Giants, managed by another legendary Irish American, John McGraw. This, the ninth World Series, was shaping up to be the most exciting yet. The Red Sox had won the first game, 4–3. The second had ended in a 6–6 tie, called after eleven innings due to darkness. Game 3 would begin at two o'clock. It would attract the largest crowd in Fenway Park's brief history: 34,624.

Outside the ballpark, mounted police in their blue-and-gold uniforms struggled mightily to corral the teeming crowds that poured off the trolleys and overwhelmed the turnstiles, while schoolboys playing hooky shinnied up lampposts, hoping to get a peek at the browning field. A brass band from the Royal Rooters, a notoriously rowdy Red Sox fan club, serenaded the cranks on Lansdowne Street a with an off-key version of "Tessie," a Broadway show tune that was the team's unofficial anthem. Scurrying everywhere were small boys in buff-colored jackets with baskets hanging from their shoulders, each yelling: "Popcorn, potater-chips, pea-nuts, and chewing gum!" The crowd was overwhelmingly male. Most refined ladies simply did not attend such noisome events. But Alice Spencer Geddes was not like most refined ladies. She was at Fenway Park that day to report on the game for the *Boston Daily Globe*, making her, in all likelihood, the first woman to cover a World Series for a major newspaper.

Alice was born in the central Massachusetts town of Athol in 1876. Her father, William Geddes, was a patent-medicine executive who spent much time overseas with her mother, Ella Ainsworth. As a result, Alice spent her formative years with her paternal grandmother, also named Alice Geddes. Much of young Alice's early life is a mystery; she later refused to discuss it. At some point she contracted polio, which left her partially paralyzed. She began attending Radcliffe in 1895 but dropped out a year later when her father died. Perhaps there were financial problems. Perhaps this is when the polio struck. She returned to the college in 1899 but never graduated.

Inspired no doubt by the muckrakers Nellie Bly and Ida Tarbell— and the need to support her mother and grandmother—she embarked on a career in journalism. In 1903 she became the publisher of the weekly *Cambridge Press*, which claimed to be the first newspaper in the United States entirely written and edited by women. A year later she moved to Wakefield, Massachusetts, and became the managing editor of the *Wakefield Citizen and Banner*. Her work was widely admired, and soon she was freelancing for the *Boston Daily Globe*. Her columns, written as "the *Globe* woman," covered a wide range of issues. She interviewed Woodrow Wilson's vice president, Thomas Marshall, and the vaudeville star Julian Eltinge, and reported on a Lawrence, Massachusetts, mill strike. And in October 1912 she found herself at game 3 of the World Series.

Her column in the next day's *Globe* appeared under the headline RED SOX AND GIANTS CHARM GLOBE WOMAN: THRILLED BY INTENSE EARNESTNESS OF WORLD'S SERIES CONTEST. Writing in the third person, she betrayed a knowledge of baseball uncommon for a woman at the time and an eye for detail uncommon for anyone at any time.

> The dark-haired, speedy, ever-watchful, modest, alert Harry Hopper has a high place in her list of heroes. She likes to watch him cover ground like a greyhound on the long hits, and when a fly is hit into his territory she instinctively cries, "He's out."

In Heine [*sic*] Wagner she finds a puzzle. He thinks and acts too rapidly for her mental process to follow him. She never knows what he is going to do next—whether he is planning a trick play or is just going to let things take their course. She gives a little cry every time he gets in the way of those glistening spikes to block a runner off the bag. She just knows he will be dreadfully spiked sometime, but she hopes it won't be until the Giants are beaten.

She likes the way Heine wears his cap pulled down over the back of his head, the side just touching his right ear. She thinks it "chic," and she notices that Lewis has copied the style, probably in admiration of his hero captain.

The Red Sox lost the game, 2–1, but went on to win the series in eight dramatic games, with the final game going ten innings. Three years later, in 1915, the Red Sox won the World Series again, but by then Alice Geddes had abandoned her newspaper work and Massachusetts for a new life in the mountains of eastern Kentucky.

If rapacious corporations are Appalachia's yang, well-intentioned do-gooders are its yin. Efforts to "civilize" and "elevate" the inhabitants of Appalachia stretch back to the first white settlers, who, expecting blissful isolation, instead found themselves hounded by itinerant preachers intent on saving them from hell.

In the early nineteenth century, another wave of do-gooders descended on the mountains: "well-bred" women from New England, bent on "uplifting" the mountaineers. This uplift movement was born in Boston, a hotbed of social activism at the time, and exported to all sections of the country. Its guiding principle was that education was the key to improvement and enlightenment. As a newspaper reporter, Alice Geddes came in contact with the movement's leaders, including the writer and activist Alice Stone Blackwell, daughter of the feminist Lucy Stone. Geddes was also a member of the Unitarian Church, which promised salvation through good works.

In February 1914 Geddes married Arthur Lloyd, a businessman whom she'd met through her newspaper work. It may have been a marriage of convenience; Geddes was thirty-eight, supporting her widowed mother, and financially ill suited to pursuing her new passion, charitable work. In the summer of 1915 the couple moved to eastern Kentucky at the invitation of the Hindman Settlement School in Knott County, a private school for mountain youth founded by two other women with good intentions, May Stone and Katherine Pettit, Kentucky natives from affluent families. (Congressman Carl Perkins was a graduate of the school.)

Alice Lloyd (as she was now known) soon struck out on her own, establishing a community center on Caney Creek, less than ten miles from the Hindman school, in a remote part of Knott County. The community center built one-room schoolhouses in neighboring communities, opened a used-clothing shop, and offered basic health care.

Lloyd named the settlement Pippa Passes after the eponymous Robert Browning play-poem, whose protagonist, a little girl named Pippa, passes through the countryside singing:

> The year's at the spring,
> And day's at the morn;
> Morning's at seven;
> The hill-side's dew-pearled;
> The lark's on the wing;
> The snail's on the thorn:
> God's in his heaven—
> All's right with the world!

The characters whom Pippa encounters are, unconsciously, compelled to perform good acts.

Alice Lloyd was unlucky in love. Her husband left her for a younger woman who worked at the community center, and in September 1918 she was left standing at the altar—literally—by another man she loved. Perhaps this is why Alice Lloyd threw herself so completely into her work. In 1923 she founded Caney Junior College, a two-year junior college awarding associate's degrees. It wasn't much to look at, just a few "roughly constructed and somewhat crude" buildings clustered along Caney Creek. Teachers were hard to recruit and even harder to retain. The Kentucky

writer James Still accepted a teaching job at the school in 1932 but left
after a day, put off by Lloyd's aloofness and the primitive facilities.

"The purpose [of the college] is to train leaders who will remain
in the mountains and serve their own people," Lloyd wrote. "A people
cannot advance farther than their leaders will take them." Students were
charged no tuition, and while the few other postsecondary schools in
the mountains emphasized vocational education, the Caney school cur-
riculum included Latin and Greek. William Hayes, a teacher hired by
Lloyd who later became the school's president, said Lloyd "saw liberal
arts preprofessional education as the way for mountain young people
to become leaders."

Lloyd could rub people the wrong way—she was a relentless self-
promoter and an aggressive fundraiser, and, according to her biographer
P. David Searles, she was "unwilling to consider views that clashed with
her own"—but she was utterly devoted to her school and its students.

Like the later generation of antipoverty workers who invaded Appalachia in the 1960s and '70s, Alice Lloyd and her do-gooding contempo-
raries were met with a mixture of gratitude, indifference, and hostility.
Some residents resented what the folklorist and writer David E. Whisnant called the "condescending middle-class missionary attitudes and
activities" that accompanied benevolent work. But P. David Searles
asserted that Alice Lloyd College "stands as living proof that the men
and women who went off to do good at the turn of the century did
indeed do good."

Alice Lloyd died on September 4, 1962. She was eighty-five. Just five
days later, the school was renamed in her honor. In 1982 Alice Lloyd
College became a four-year college awarding bachelor's degrees.

Today the campus resembles most other small colleges, save for its
verticality. The school is in a hollow eighteen hundred feet deep and
just five hundred feet across, so a walk across campus is more akin to a
mountain hike. At the center of campus still stands one of the "roughly
constructed and somewhat crude" buildings that was erected when Alice
Lloyd founded the college in 1923. Known as the Founder's Shack, it
is a poignant relic symbolizing the great strides that the college—and
Appalachia—have made over the last century.

21

7:00 PM—Pippa Passes, Reverend Baldridge

LAWRENCE BALDRIDGE WAS ONE OF THE MANY CANEY STUDENTS whose lives were shaped by Alice Lloyd and the college she founded, and he personifies her ideal of training leaders who will "remain in the mountains and serve their own people."

When I met him in the summer of 2018, he was, at eighty-one, still the full-time pastor at Caney Baptist Church, just down Highway 899 from the school. His wife, Martha—they wed in 1963—still plays piano at worship services and teaches Sunday school (and does "much, much more," he tells me). Except for a brief tenure teaching high school in Cincinnati in the late 1950s and early '60s, Baldridge has lived his entire life in the mountains, and he's been the pastor at Caney Baptist since 1964. Tall and thin, he still looks like the basketball player he once was, and he continues to follow the game closely. (If anything unites the two disparate halves of Kentucky, the bluegrass and the mountains, it's a shared love of basketball.) Reverend Baldridge attended Caney Junior College when Alice Lloyd was still in charge, and he was instrumental in bringing Robert Kennedy to speak at the school in February 1968.

We met in the church's fellowship hall, which is attached to the church. Both were built by a volunteer group called Carpenters for Christ and opened in 2009, after a years-long capital campaign that included many fish fries and spaghetti dinners. We sat in folding chairs at a long banquet table beneath bright fluorescent lights.

Baldridge's father was a coal miner, his mother a housewife. They had four children. Lawrence, born in Floyd County in 1936, was the youngest. He was raised in a very religious home. His parents were both Old Regular Baptists, a common denomination in eastern Kentucky. Old Regular Baptists trace their roots to the early decades of the nineteenth century, when furious debates over the particulars of predestination, proselytizing, and atonement splintered Baptists into innumerable factions. Old Regulars shun innovations that "new" Baptists have long embraced: Sunday school (because it inserts man into the "nurturing process"), trained clergy (because preaching cannot be taught; it is a gift from God), and evangelizing (because only God can save your soul). Their marathon services combine frenzied preaching with mournful-sounding hymns sung in a peculiar style called lined-out hymnody, a kind of call-and-response singing that dates back to seventeenth-century Britain and was born of the high level of illiteracy and the prohibitive cost of books.

At nineteen, however, Lawrence Baldridge felt called to spread the Good News of Jesus Christ, so he joined a Southern Baptist church. Mission work is something the Old Regulars frown upon. "That was really hard on my parents," he says, "because they thought there was nothing else but Old Regular Baptists. When I broke from that and became a Missionary Baptist, as we're called here in the mountains—they'd never known anything like that."

When Baldridge graduated from high school in tiny Garrett, Kentucky, in 1953, he wanted to go to college, but his parents couldn't afford to send him. Tuition-free Caney Junior College was his only option. He was accepted and excelled. When he graduated with an associate's degree in 1955, he was awarded a Caney Cottage Scholarship to attend the University of Kentucky and live rent-free in Caney Cottage, a dorm for Caney graduates on the UK campus. He earned a bachelor's degree in education and a master's in social work from UK, as well as master's degrees from the University of Louisville (in community development) and Southern Baptist Theological Seminary (in divinity). Over the decades he has traveled the world as a missionary, but he always returns to the mountains, where his contributions to the region's cultural and religious life are incalculable. In 2011 he was named Alice Lloyd College Alumnus of the Year. He golfs regularly and can shoot his age occasionally. He plays guitar ("mostly Johnny Cash and John Denver songs"), and he writes a poem a day, one of which is this book's epigraph.

In 1967, shortly after the Supreme Court's *Loving* decision struck down state laws banning interracial marriage, Lawrence Baldridge was the first minister to marry an interracial couple in Knott County and, perhaps, in all of Kentucky. "I did, I got some calls the night before, death threats, and I thought I would be shot. I woke my kids up before I left, and I told them that we were having an outside wedding and I might be shot. But what I'm doing, I'm doing because I think blacks and whites should be equal. And if I did not perform the ceremony I would be saying that one was less equal than the other.

"Before I went over, I called the state police and told them to come by where the wedding was, and there was all those bushes up on the hill, and I expected at any time for a shot to come out of those bushes. Because several people were incensed that I had agreed to do that. So the state police came. There were two African American state policemen, and they were both about six five with a pistol on the side, so I thought we were safe then."

Baldridge led campaigns to end strip mining in the mountains, and in 1982 he led the opposition to a referendum that would have legalized the sale of alcohol in Knott County. (The measure failed by a vote of 4,516 to 1,608, and the county is still dry.) He is opposed to abortion and considers himself a pro-life liberal. "The left took it too fast," he says. "Human rights are human rights and should be human rights. That's what the Constitution's about. But on the other hand, there's a sense in which, until people are ready, they will react to your forcing them to do anything. Here in east Kentucky, I think this is why they voted overwhelmingly for Trump. Because of the abortion issue and because of the gay rights issue and because, I think, there might've been a bit of the black issue too, with Obama. But I think Obama was a gentleman and a scholar and a very good president."

When he enrolled at Caney Junior College in 1953, Alice Lloyd was an old woman, bedridden much of the time, still partially paralyzed. But she remained a formidable presence and ran the school with an iron fist. "I knew her," Baldridge says. "I was afraid of her. I was a student. Like all guys, I got away with what I could. So she called me in a couple times and put the fear of the Lord in me. Also, she saw something in me. She was almost a psychiatrist or psychologist. She could see you and listen to you and probe you and find out about you."

In the winter of 1967–68, Lawrence Baldridge was teaching English at Alice Lloyd College. In early February, when word got out that Kennedy was coming to visit the area, Balridge took it upon himself to invite the senator to speak at the school. He'd started an informal speakers series—Harry Caudill had given a talk—and he thought Kennedy would be perfect for it. He called Kennedy's offices in New York and Washington. Finally, he was put through to the senator's traveling secretary, who told him to put the request in writing. He did, and less than two weeks later Robert Kennedy showed up in Pippa Passes.

———————

After a hot meal of beef stew in the student canteen, Kennedy stepped back out into the cold night air and walked a short distance up a steep hill to the school's assembly hall, Cushing Hall, where some 250 students were waiting for him, seated on folding chairs set up on the floor or standing shoulder to shoulder in the small balcony that ringed the room. Most of the young men wore jackets and ties. Most of the young women wore sweaters over their blouses. William Hayes, who'd succeeded Alice Lloyd as the college's president upon her death six years earlier, introduced Kennedy. It was approaching eight o'clock now, and Kennedy had traveled about two hundred miles all over eastern Kentucky that day. He was exhausted, but an audience of young people always energized him, and as he took his place behind the lectern on the stage, he appeared to rejuvenate.

"The place was full, and they were hanging off the rafters when he came," Lawrence Baldridge remembers. "And he just come in from

The audience in Cushing Hall for Kennedy's remarks at Alice Lloyd College, February 13, 1968. *Berea College Special Collections and Archives, Berea, Kentucky*

being all day long with people. So he came on over here and he was so tired that his arms were limp. I mean, his whole body was just limp as a rag. And he got up and started speaking, and he kinda livened up because of the audience."

I ask Reverend Baldridge if anybody had recorded the event. "Sure," he says. "Bennie Moore has the tape." Bennie Moore was an Alice Lloyd teacher who was not in attendance that night. But a few months later he needed to borrow the school's reel-to-reel tape recorder. It was stored in Cushing Hall. A tape was already loaded on the machine. It was a recording of the Kennedy event. Moore took it home for safekeeping, and he still has it. (He gave a copy to the school.) I called him and asked if I could get a copy. He said sure. His son uploaded the recording to Dropbox that night.

"I'm delighted to be here," Kennedy began, "and very pleased to see all of you and very grateful for the hospitality of this college, picking up a couple of strangers traveling through the evening and finding a meal for them and giving them a room to sleep in. Very grateful for that."*

Listening to the tape today, one is struck by the lack of anger, sarcasm, and self-aggrandizement throughout. Kennedy never answered a question until he was certain he understood it. More than once he asked a questioner, "What do you mean?" Kennedy and his young interlocutors were subdued and serious, though the senator occasionally cracked a self-deprecating joke. He told the students they needed to work hard: "When I went to work at the Department of Justice, I worked as an ordinary lawyer receiving the lowest possible salary. And that was in 1951. And then I worked very, very hard and I was diligent. And then ten years later I was made attorney general."

In his brief opening remarks, Kennedy stressed the importance of education.

> Without people with education, this section is going to continue to suffer. People with education, however, can make a major difference. There's great wealth here. Great possibilities in eastern Kentucky. But there has to be people who are going out to fight for eastern Kentucky. That's what really is desperately needed. People who are going—not only in the Congress of the United States but also in every walk of life—people who are going to get up and stand on their feet and fight for eastern Kentucky: that's what is needed.

He mentioned two unemployed miners he'd met on his travels earlier that day, neither of whom had more than a third-grade education.

> You are the most exclusive minority in the world, because you have a college education. You have this advanced training that very, very few of the citizens of this world have. And with that

---

* Worth noting, if only for its peculiarity, is Robert Kennedy's pronunciation of "Appalachia." He said it app-uh-LAY-chee-uh. The correct way to say the word is a matter of fierce, sometimes hostile debate. Generally speaking, in upper Appalachia (roughly from Pennsylvania northward) it's app-uh-LAY-chuh (or -shuh). Less common in that region is Kennedy's pronunciation. From West Virginia on down (including, emphatically, eastern Kentucky), it's app-uh-LATCH-uh.

great opportunity comes a great responsibility. And that's a responsibility to those who are far less well off. And desperately need your helping hand. And you can make a difference. One person can make a difference.

Several times Kennedy asked the students for their opinion by a show of hands. *Should we stop the bombing in North Vietnam or stay the course? Do you support strip mining or oppose it?* Kennedy never called his political opponents names or questioned their patriotism. "He wanted dialogue between the students and himself," Baldridge says. "He didn't want to just give a speech. He gave a short speech and then he opened it up for questions."

Larry Hayes was skeptical of Kennedy's motives. Hayes was twenty years old and in his second year at Alice Lloyd. He was sitting in the third row of the auditorium for Kennedy's speech. "I was convinced he was just using us for a political prop," Hayes remembers. "Lyndon Johnson had come down here [to eastern Kentucky in 1964], hopping around in his helicopter, but nothing had changed. And I was convinced it was going to be the same way with Kennedy. Just using us."

But when Kennedy walked onto the stage, Hayes immediately noticed something about him. "His shoes were dirty. They were all scratched up and muddy, and it really made an impression on me. This man had gotten out of the car, he'd walked in the mud. He had empathy." While Hayes did not become a Kennedy supporter on the spot, his respect for the senator grew immensely. "Up on the stage, I could look directly at those shoes. I'll never forget that."

While some college campuses were in turmoil at the time, Alice Lloyd's was not—although Larry Hayes remembers one classmate who was a hippie. Still, Hayes says, the students were no less concerned about the day's pressing issues than their peers on other, more famous campuses. "We'd have bull sessions in our rooms just about every night," he says. "We talked about Vietnam a lot." When he graduated with his associate's degree in the spring, Hayes would lose his student deferment, and he was worried. "I couldn't afford to go to UK to get my bachelor's," he recalls. "So I knew there was a good chance I'd be drafted."

Vietnam was on the minds of many Alice Lloyd students that night. When Kennedy opened the floor to questions, the first came from a young woman who asked, "In our dorm we've been anticipating your arrival, and the one thing that everybody wanted to know was your stand on Vietnam."

Kennedy laughed. "Oh God!" he said. "Should I send you a copy of my speech?"

22

The Deepening Swamp

FIVE DAYS EARLIER, ON FEBRUARY 8, with the full fury of North Vietnam's Tet Offensive launched in late January now apparent, Robert Kennedy had given a speech in Chicago in which he called Vietnam "the deepening swamp" and declared "the time has come to take a new look at the war." American soldiers were dying in unprecedented numbers. In fact, with American troops and their allies fighting bitterly to recapture cities lost to the North Vietnamese in the offensive, the week of February 11–17, 1968, would be the deadliest week of the war for US forces, with 543 Americans killed and another 2,547 wounded.

In his Chicago speech—which some have called the Unwinnable War speech—Kennedy criticized the corrupt South Vietnamese government's seemingly half-hearted commitment to the war effort. "We have an ally in name only," he said. "We support a government without supporters." He added, "The current regime in Saigon is unwilling or incapable of being an effective ally in the war against Communists." Although he never mentioned the president's name, Kennedy's speech was interpreted as a broadside against Lyndon Johnson, with the *New York Times* noting that it "attacked . . . every important facet of the Johnson Administration's policy in Vietnam." Kennedy, however, continued to insist he had no intention of challenging Johnson for the Democratic presidential nomination.

On February 14, American and South Vietnamese forces inched their way toward recapturing Huế, the third-largest city in the Republic of South Vietnam. After a day of ferocious fighting, they succeeded in gaining just two hundred yards.

Meanwhile, another bloody battle was raging about one hundred miles north of Huế: the Battle of Quảng Trị. Like Huế, Quảng Trị City had been captured by the North Vietnamese during Tet. Also like Huế, Quảng Trị was an ancient city with a fortified citadel at its center. This made the fighting in both cities especially intense, some of the fiercest hand-to-hand combat of the war.

On the afternoon of Friday, February 16, a Marine from Letcher County, Jimmy Ellison Tolliver, was killed when his helicopter was shot down outside Quảng Trị City. At twenty-eight, Tolliver was considerably older than the average front-line soldier in Vietnam.*

Born in 1940 in the tiny hamlet of Haymond, Kentucky (though its post office, for reasons unclear, is named Cromona), Tolliver enlisted in the Marines in 1964 and rose quickly to the rank of staff sergeant. He arrived in Vietnam in July 1967 and was a door gunner with the First Marine Aircraft Wing on a UH-1, the helicopter commonly known as a Huey.

On February 16, Tolliver was part of a crew assigned to extract an eight-man reconnaissance team trapped behind enemy lines six miles northwest of Đông Hà. What happened next is detailed in his Silver Star citation.

> Arriving over the designated area, he expertly directed a heavy volume of machine gun fire on the enemy positions during repeated strafing runs in support of the extraction aircraft. Although five Marines had been extracted, subsequent attempts to rescue the remaining men had failed due to a heavy volume

---

* In his 1985 hit song "19," the British composer Paul Hardcastle codified the myth that the average age of a combat soldier in Vietnam was nineteen. The average age of a combat soldier in any war is difficult to ascertain. However, the average age of the 58,148 Americans killed in Vietnam was twenty-three, and the average age of the 40,934 Americans killed in combat, perhaps a better measure of the average age of a combat soldier, was twenty-two.

of ground fire which had seriously damaged three helicopters. When his pilot volunteered to evacuate the surrounded men and made an approach to the hazardous area, the aircraft was damaged by hostile fire and forced to abort the approach. Realizing the seriousness of the situation, he again provided a heavy volume of machine gun fire during his helicopter's second attempt and, after landing, continued to deliver covering fire, enabling the three Marines to embark. Lifting from the fire-swept site, his aircraft was struck by a burst of enemy fire and crashed, mortally wounding Staff Sergeant Tolliver.

All ten Marines aboard the Huey were killed. Their bodies were later recovered. Jimmy Tolliver is buried in a small cemetery in Ermine, about ten miles down the road from Haymond and not far from Whitesburg. His headstone erroneously gives his date of death as February 6, 1968. Tolliver was survived by his wife and their three young children.

Jimmy Tolliver was just one of 1,056 Kentuckians to die in the war, a disproportionate share of whom hailed from the eastern half of the state, including twenty-two from Harlan County and fourteen from Letcher. Per capita, Appalachia lost more sons in the Vietnam War than any other region of the United States. West Virginia's death rate was the highest of any state, and it's been estimated that eastern Kentucky's was even higher.

Eastern Kentucky has a long history of military valor. During the First World War, Breathitt County was said to be the only county in the nation that was never compelled to hold a draft. The county met its draft quotas wholly with volunteers. Love of country is one factor. But young men from Appalachia have been willing to fight and die for their country for reasons far beyond pure patriotism. The military has long offered an escape from the drudgery of mountain living, an alternative to a lifetime stooped in the coal mines, work inherently dangerous in its own right. It has afforded otherwise unimaginable opportunities for travel, education, employment, and adventure.

Especially valued for their marksmanship and familiarity with mountainous terrain, soldiers from Appalachia were often assigned—or volunteered—to walk point on patrols in Vietnam, which accounts in part for their unusually high casualty rate.

"Appalachians make good soldiers, and the Army knows it," Steven Giles, a VA psychologist, told the *Baltimore Sun* in 1991. Giles researched the phenomenon and even came up with a name for it: Sergeant York syndrome. Alvin York was born in 1887 in the mountains of Pall Mall, Tennessee, less than ten miles south of the Kentucky line. As a corporal in the Meuse-Argonne campaign of the First World War, he "charged with great daring a machine gun nest which was pouring deadly and incessant fire upon his platoon." In taking the machine gun nest, York killed at least 25 German soldiers and captured 132 more, including 4 officers. For his heroism he was promoted to sergeant and, after the war, awarded the Medal of Honor. York became the archetype of the mountaineer turned soldier. Gary Cooper won an Oscar for his portrayal of York in a 1941 biopic that inspired countless young men to enlist in the armed forces after Pearl Harbor.

Appalachians' reputation for valor in Vietnam was hard earned. Although they accounted for only about 8 percent of all troops, Appalachians won 13 percent of the war's Medals of Honor.

Appalachian mothers and fathers were rightly proud of their children fighting Communism in Vietnam. But like many loyal Americans they harbored grave doubts about the war. "Our area is feeding the war machine," one disgruntled parent told Kennedy in Kentucky. "Our boys have been taught the art of killing. They aren't genteel enough for draft dodging."

The Alice Lloyd student who questioned Kennedy about Vietnam said she and her friends had been discussing his Chicago speech but were still unclear whether he preferred pulling out or changing tactics.

"Mostly the latter," he answered.

> I'm opposed to unilaterally withdrawing from Vietnam. I think that would be a great mistake. I think it would weaken not only the prestige and position of the United States in Southeast Asia, but I think it would have an adverse effect on our relationship with other countries all over the globe. . . . This is a war by the South Vietnamese. We can go in and help them. We can assist them in many, many ways. And there are areas, perhaps, in which we can guide them. But we can't win the war for them. In

the last analysis this is their struggle. This is their war. And they have to be interested in it and committed to it themselves. . . . And the fact is the government of South Vietnam is corrupt. Many of them, including their generals, are making huge profits out of this struggle. The corruption permeates every aspect of life and every aspect of society within South Vietnam. . . . I'm opposed to United States troops doing all of the fighting and all of the dying. . . . Why is it necessary for American troops to go into Saigon to throw the Viet Cong out, or the North Vietnamese? Why don't the South Vietnamese throw them out? Or in Huế? Why does it always have to be American troops that do the fighting? . . . Why is it Americans up at Khe Sanh tonight, in that very critical and crucial battle, why isn't it South Vietnamese that are holding that spot? Why should it be Americans all the time? And that's what I object to. It shouldn't just be an American war. We can help them. But they should be able and willing to carry the struggle themselves. That's what I object to.

23

"Ulysses"

"ONE OF THE BIG CONCERNS in this area is strip mining," a male Alice Lloyd student said to Kennedy. "This takes a lot of the wealth out of the region and also ruins the beauty of the land. What do you think, if any, kind of federal legislation can be done to improve this?"

"Well," Kennedy answered, "it seems to me that the state of Kentucky should be able to deal with this themselves. Shouldn't they? I mean, it might be that federal legislation is necessary, but the state of Kentucky could pass laws dealing with strip mining very easily, couldn't they?" Here the audience chuckled knowingly—in Kentucky, laws regulating strip mining could never be passed very easily.

"Well," Kennedy added sheepishly, "I mean, it's possible and it's constitutional." Here the audience burst into laughter.

Near the end of the evening, Lawrence Baldridge, the Alice Lloyd teacher who'd invited Kennedy to campus, raised his hand. "I'd like to ask a question, Senator Kennedy, about yourself in relation to your deep concern, apparently, for people who have poverty," Baldridge said. "All of us have experienced it very much, and I would say that probably you have not. And yet you have a deep, deep concern, it seems to me, for people who have poverty. So where does this come from, what's the source of it? I'm interested as a person to find this out about you."

Kennedy was silent for several seconds, as were the students who awaited his answer, and the hall fell quiet. For the first time all day,

Rev. Lawrence Baldridge, photographed at Caney Baptist Church in Pippa Passes, Kentucky, February 2019. *Lou Murrey*

Robert Kennedy was at a loss for words. Finally, he said: "Oh, I don't know what, I don't know. I don't, uh, I don't, uh. That's a great answer [*laughter*]. I just don't have the—I don't know what the answer to that is." Then in a barely audible voice: "I'm sorry."

Fifty years later, Lawrence Baldridge chokes up as he recalls the exchange. "Had he said anything else, I'd've known it was false," he tells me. "What he was saying to me was basically, *I came because I want to bring equality to people. I want to do social good for this world.* That's what I heard."

"If more politicians knew poetry, and more poets knew politics," John Kennedy said in 1958, "I am convinced the world would be a little better place to live."

Robert Kennedy shared his brother's conviction. Kennedy was known to keep slim volumes of poetry in the inside pocket of his suit jacket, handy for reading in rare moments of quiet, free of the demands of family and politics. He loved poetry, and he frequently quoted verse, often spontaneously, in his public remarks. He concluded his first speech after his brother's assassination, at a St. Patrick's Day dinner in Scranton, Pennsylvania, with lines from "Lament for the Death of Eoghan Ruadh O'Neill," Thomas Davis's requiem for the Irish hero:

> Sheep without a shepherd, when the snow shuts
>   out the sky—
> Oh! why did you leave us, Eoghan? Why did you
>   die?

In his unscripted comments in Indianapolis the night Martin Luther King Jr. was assassinated, he quoted Aeschylus, from memory: "In our sleep, pain which cannot forget falls drop by drop upon the heart until, in our own despair, against our will, comes wisdom through the awful grace of God."

The title of Kennedy's 1967 book *To Seek a Newer World* was taken from Alfred, Lord Tennyson's "Ulysses": "Come, my friends, / 'Tis not too late to seek a newer world."

"Ulysses" was also the poem that Kennedy quoted at the conclusion of his talk with the students at Alice Lloyd College, sending them into the night with these lines:

> How dull it is to pause, to make an end,
> To rust unburnish'd, not to shine in use!
> As tho' to breathe were life!

"That's really what's involved in this," he told the students.

> You can just pass through this existence and pass through life and not have made a difference. Or we can try to change the course—maybe not change the course of our whole country but change the course and change the lives of many, many people. And you have a special responsibility and obligation to do that. And in my judgment you also have a special chance, a special

opportunity. So I think if all of us meet our responsibilities—you here, and those of us who are in the Congress of the United States—if all of us make that kind of common effort, it seems to me it will benefit the people of eastern Kentucky who so desperately need it. Thank you very much.

Kennedy spent the night on the Alice Lloyd campus, in the home of the college's vice president.

A few weeks later, Larry Hayes, the second-year student who was due to lose his college deferment, received a letter notifying him that he'd been awarded a Caney Cottage Scholarship to attend the University of Kentucky. He wouldn't be going to Vietnam after all. He's now a beloved social studies teacher in Knott County, another example of Alice Lloyd's ideal of training leaders who will "remain in the mountains and serve their own people."

24

Campaign '68

Robert Kennedy's trip included all the elements of an election campaign: press conferences, speeches on courthouse steps, meetings with local government and party officials, and photo ops galore. "The tour was billed as a field hearing on rural poverty," wrote William Greider in the *Louisville Courier-Journal*. "But at times it had all the flavor and trappings of a candidate's campaign swing through the district." Added Richard Harwood in the *Washington Post*, "Sen. Robert F. Kennedy (D–N.Y.) discovered Eastern Kentucky Tuesday and it was almost like the circus had hit town."

Kennedy would not formally announce his candidacy for the Democratic presidential nomination until March 16, but his two days in eastern Kentucky, February 13–14, were intended in part to test how his campaign themes—racial justice, fighting poverty, ending American involvement in Vietnam—would resonate with rural white voters.

Also hoping to woo those very same voters was another presidential candidate, one whose approach was the opposite of Kennedy's on practically every issue.

On the morning of Thursday, February 8, 1968—the same day Kennedy delivered his famous Unwinnable War speech in Chicago—George

Wallace, a forty-eight-year-old onetime boxing champion and former governor of Alabama, announced his candidacy for the presidency of the United States at a press conference in Washington. Nominally a Democrat, Wallace announced he would run as the candidate for a third party founded just for him: the American Independent Party.*

Standing before a dozen television cameras and about seventy-five reporters in the Cotillion Room of the Sheraton-Park Hotel (now the Washington Marriott Wardman Park), and wearing a new pair of Goldwater-style black-framed eyeglasses, Wallace read a bland three-page statement, stumbling over the words several times. He seemed uncharacteristically subdued—one reporter said he seemed almost grim—until it was time to take questions. When a reporter asked him what he thought of Florida governor Claude Kirk, a Republican who claimed Wallace had made a secret deal with President Johnson to run as a third-party candidate to split the Republican vote and ensure Johnson's reelection, Wallace just rolled his eyes and twirled his right index finger beside his right temple, leaving no doubt that he thought Kirk was crazy.

He blamed "activists, anarchists, revolutionaries, and Communists" for fomenting unrest in cities and on college campuses: "I would keep the peace if I had to keep 30,000 troops on the streets, two feet apart and with two-foot-long bayonets." He pilloried bureaucrats, and claimed overregulation was stifling business: "I would bring all these briefcase-toting bureaucrats in the Department of Health, Education and Welfare to Washington and throw their briefcases in the Potomac River." He claimed "so-called civil rights laws" were "an attack on the property rights of this country and on the free enterprise system and local government."

And he railed, somewhat bizarrely, against the forced integration of public showers: "No wonder we're not winning the war in Vietnam," he said. "Everyone is down in Birmingham, Ala[bama], checking the

---

* Although continually roiled by internal disputes, the American Independent Party soldiers on as a fringe party on the far right that bills itself as "the party of ordered liberty in a nation under God." The AIP is the largest third party in California, though a 2016 *Los Angeles Times* survey found that 73 percent of the voters who registered with the party mistakenly believed they were registering as independent voters, i.e., independent of all political parties.

shower stalls trying to find out who is showering with one another. They've checked every shower stall in every textile mill in the state."

"I am in the race irrevocably," he announced. "I will run to win. I fully think we can win." Privately, however, he admitted his only hope was to win enough electoral votes to deny the other candidates a majority and throw the election into the House of Representatives.

Toward the end of the press conference, Wallace was asked about his wife, Lurleen, who had recently completed four weeks of radiation therapy for a recurrence of cancer. "Our hope and prayer is that the radiation will arrest her problem," Wallace said.

At the moment, Lurleen Wallace was more than George Wallace's wife. Technically, she was also his boss, for Lurleen was the governor of Alabama and George was merely her "advisor."

25

Lurleen

THERE WERE SO MANY TRAGEDIES in the spring of 1968 that the agonizing demise of Lurleen Wallace, the incumbent governor of Alabama, barely registered beyond the state's borders at the time and is all but forgotten today. But her death was no less a tragedy than King's and Kennedy's, if only because it was the result not of an assassin's bullet but of a husband's unimaginable cruelty and neglect.

Robert Kennedy was far from the perfect husband. His friend and aide Richard Goodwin said there was no doubt that Kennedy had extramarital affairs. "Of course he did," Goodwin told Kennedy biographer Larry Tye. "That's a Kennedy family tradition." But Kennedy's infidelity pales when compared to Wallace's mistreatment of his wife, whose premature death was at least partly his fault.

Lurleen Burns was born in Tuscaloosa County on September 19, 1926. She graduated from high school at fifteen, too young to enroll in nursing school, as was her dream. To bide her time, she took a job at the Kresge's five-and-dime in Tuscaloosa, which is where she met George Corley Wallace Jr., a recent graduate of the University of Alabama School of Law soon to be inducted into the Army Air Corps. They were married on May 22, 1943. She was sixteen. He was twenty-four.

In 1961 the couple's fourth and final child, a girl named Janie Lee, was born by Cesarean section. Shortly after the birth, the doctor who performed the C-section informed George that he'd noticed some abnormal tissue during the procedure. He suspected Lurleen had uterine cancer, and he urged George to send her to an oncologist. As was not unusual at the time, the doctor never spoke with Lurleen about his concerns—only her husband.

George Wallace had already lost his first run for governor, in 1958. Back then he'd run as a moderate; he was even endorsed by the NAACP. His opponent in the Democratic runoff—the de facto election—was John Patterson, a hard-line segregationist endorsed by the Ku Klux Klan. After losing to Patterson by eleven points, Wallace swore that he would never be "out-niggered" again.

Wallace was planning on running for governor again in 1962, and Lurleen's condition would, well, complicate his campaign—so he didn't tell her she possibly had cancer.

The Alabama constitution prohibited governors from serving consecutive terms, so John Patterson was barred from running for reelection in '62. Wallace—running as a staunch segregationist this time—won the Democratic runoff with 55 percent of the vote. The Republicans didn't even bother to field a candidate in the general election, which Wallace won with 96 percent. In his inaugural address on January 14, 1963, he vowed to block federal attempts to integrate Alabama's schools, famously declaring, "Segregation now, segregation tomorrow, segregation forever."

In early 1963, three African American students applied to the University of Alabama. Wallace promised to block their admission. Mindful of the rioting precipitated by the integration of the University of Mississippi the previous fall and desperate to prevent a repeat in Tuscaloosa, Robert Kennedy, the attorney general, flew to Montgomery—the "Cradle of the Confederacy"—on the evening of Wednesday, April 24, 1963. He met with Wallace in the governor's office at nine o'clock the next morning. Kennedy called it a "courtesy call."

Although the two men had been born into starkly different circumstances—Wallace's father, George C. Wallace Sr., was a dirt-poor cotton farmer who died when George Jr. was just eighteen—Kennedy and Wallace had much in common. Both were slightly built (Kennedy was five nine, Wallace five seven), and both were consumed with a need to prove themselves. Unlike his two older, more athletic brothers,

Joe Jr. and Jack, Robert managed to letter in football at Harvard. As a teenager, George Wallace twice won Alabama's Golden Gloves bantamweight championship. What his biographer Stephan Lesher wrote of Wallace—"the willingness to expose himself to risk in the pursuit of personal achievement; a combination of confrontational scrappiness with a frank recognition of his own limitations; and a shrewd ability to assess an opponent's strengths and weaknesses"—could just as easily be said of Kennedy.

The timing of the meeting in the governor's office was inauspicious. Thirteen days earlier, on April 12, 1963—Good Friday—Martin Luther King Jr. had been arrested for protesting segregation in Birmingham. Four days later, King composed his famous Letter from Birmingham Jail. And on April 23, just two days before the meeting, William Lewis Moore, a white postal worker from Baltimore, was murdered while walking along US Highway 11 near the town of Attalla in northern Alabama. Moore was on a quixotic and foolhardy one-man protest march from Chattanooga, Tennessee, to Jackson, Mississippi, where he planned to deliver a letter to Governor Ross Barnett protesting segregation. He wore signs reading END SEGREGATION IN AMERICA and EQUAL RIGHTS FOR ALL (MISSISSIPPI OR BUST). Moore was shot twice in the head at close range with a .22-caliber rifle. The weapon was traced to a white man named Floyd Simpson, but a grand jury refused to indict him and he was never tried for the murder. Officially the crime is still unsolved.

Wallace began the meeting by telling Kennedy that he would be tape-recording their conversation to "avoid misunderstandings," and he asked Kennedy to speak up because "I don't hear good." Wallace was partially deaf, the result of spinal meningitis contracted when he was in the army, and he habitually cupped his hand behind his ear.

"The federal courts rewrote the law in the matter of integration and segregation," Wallace complained to Kennedy. "For a hundred years they said we could have segregated schools, and then all of a sudden, for political reasons, they pull the rug out from under us." The meeting lasted eighty minutes. Kennedy and Wallace would achieve no rapprochement and would remain implacable adversaries. "Neither man gave an inch," the *Montgomery Advertiser* reported the next day.

But in the end, Wallace knew he could not stand up to the might of the federal government—and Kennedy knew he had to let Wallace save face. So, on June 11, Wallace made his famous Stand in the Schoolhouse Door to prevent two of the black students, James Hood and Vivian Malone, from registering for classes at Alabama. But it was purely political theater, with the final act agreed upon in advance. White crayon markings on the pavement showed Wallace where to stand, and he wore a microphone for the benefit of the radio and television crews carefully positioned beforehand. Then, after Wallace finished speaking and the crews packed up their gear and left, Hood and Malone registered without incident.

In 1965 Lurleen finally learned she had cancer—and that her husband had known but never told her. She was, according to George Wallace biographer Dan T. Carter, "outraged." Her husband's excuse for not telling her did nothing to abate her anger. "Now honey," he said, "there was no point in you worrying about that."

Nonetheless, the following year, she agreed to participate in a remarkable political charade. Since George was barred by the Alabama constitution from running for a second consecutive term as governor in 1966, Lurleen ran as his surrogate. She announced her candidacy in a "rip-snorting rally" in the chambers of the state house of representatives on February 24, 1966. If elected, she said in a prepared five-paragraph statement, she would "let George do it" when it came to matters of state policy. "My election would enable my husband to carry on his programs for the people of Alabama." Then George took the podium to deliver a twenty-five-minute harangue in which he promised to expel from Alabama's public schools any students who "sign petitions, raise clothes, money, or blood for the Viet Cong." At the press conference afterward, only George, not Lurleen, fielded questions.

Lurleen handily won the primary and general elections and was sworn into office on Monday, January 16, 1967, becoming Alabama's first female governor and just the third woman to serve as a state's chief executive. In her inaugural address she hinted at George's presidential ambitions, saying she entered the race for governor "for the purpose of permitting my husband to take our fight [for states' rights] to the final court of appeal—the people of the United States in whom rests the ultimate sovereign power of this nation."

"Looking like a first-place winner in a Gallup poll of the nation's 10 best dressed women," Montgomery's *Alabama Journal* noted, "an all-in-black Lurleen B. Wallace waved to thousands upon thousands of cheering Alabamians this morning as she rode to take her place of honor on a flag-draped reviewing stand in front of the State Capitol." Lurleen Wallace was forty years old and, unbeknownst to most Alabamans, dying of cancer.

Although less conspicuously racist than her husband, Lurleen did nothing to alter his pro-segregation policies. "Statehouse reporters . . . have made it clear that when they speak of 'the Governor,' they don't mean Lurleen," a reporter noted shortly after she took office.

As First Gentleman of Alabama, George Wallace could not only continue to implement his policies as de facto governor; he could also use state resources to fund his presidential ambitions. One of his full-time campaign workers, Ed Ewing, was on the Alabama payroll as Lurleen's

Alabama governor Lurleen Wallace in her official portrait, 1967. *Alabama Department of Archives and History*

press secretary. About twenty state employees worked for the campaign full time, and everywhere he went he was accompanied by a contingent of Alabama state troopers acting as bodyguards.

In June 1967, Lurleen announced that she would be entering the renowned MD Anderson Hospital in Houston for treatment of a "malignancy which may . . . require surgery." But the Alabama constitution prohibited governors from being outside the state for more than twenty consecutive days, so in the midst of her treatment Lurleen was periodically required to return to Alabama; otherwise she would lose the governorship and George would lose his free campaign staff.

Lurleen's last public appearance was at an American Independent Party event in Houston on January 11, 1968. By then the cancer had spread to her colon and pelvis, but George was too busy campaigning to spend much time with his sick wife. In April the popular *Parade* magazine gossip columnist Walter Scott (real name: Lloyd Shearer) addressed the issue succinctly in his usual question-and-answer format:

Q. Lurleen Wallace and her cancer. The whole nation has known it. What sort of man is her husband who instead of spending as much time with his wife in her dwindling days, has spent it electioneering for the presidency? E.R., Mobile, Ala.
A. George Wallace has always been an ambitious man.

By late April the cancer had spread to her liver and lungs and she weighed less than eighty pounds. Lurleen Wallace died on May 7, 1968. George Wallace farmed out his four children to friends or relatives so he could continue his presidential campaign. He would marry two more times.

Although they had come to occupy two distant points on the political spectrum, Robert Kennedy and George Wallace were both competing for the same group of voters in 1968: rural whites, mostly poor, troubled by the monumental social and cultural changes taking place in the nation. Kennedy hoped to win them over with empathy and compassion. Wallace had a different strategy.

Four years earlier, in 1964, George Wallace had briefly run for the Democratic presidential nomination. Running an openly racist campaign, he had managed to win nearly 30 percent of the vote in the

Indiana primary. Four years later, Kennedy ran in the Indiana primary on a civil rights platform and won it with 42 percent. Surely many of the rural white Hoosiers who had voted for Wallace in 1964 also voted for Kennedy in 1968. Both candidates appealed to them, albeit in starkly different ways. The NBC News correspondent Charles Quinn remembered a conversation he had with a white voter in Gary, Indiana, in 1968.

> Q. Well, what do you think of Kennedy?
> A. We like Kennedy very much . . .
> Q. But I understand you're not terribly crazy about Negroes.
> A. Naw, don't like Negroes. Nobody around here likes Negroes.
> Q. Here's a man who stands for helping the Negro, and you say you don't like them. How can you vote for him?
> A. I don't know. Just like him . . .

"All these whites," Quinn wrote, "all these blue-collar people and ethnic people who supported Kennedy . . . felt that [he] would really do what he thought was right for the black people but, at the same time, would not tolerate lawlessness and violence. The Kennedy toughness came through on that. They were willing to gamble . . . because they knew in their hearts that the country was not right. . . . They were willing to gamble on this man, maybe, who would try to keep things within reasonable order; and at the same time, do some of the things that they knew really should be done."

In 1968 George Wallace called himself the "angry man's candidate," and his campaign slogan was "Stand Up for America." Robert Kennedy campaigned with what one writer called a "peculiar fierce compassion [that] spoke to hardscrabble farmers as much as poor black mothers."

On March 21, 1968, Kennedy returned to Wallace's home state to give a speech at the University of Alabama. "Negroes are helping fight for freedom in Vietnam, and we want them to find the doors of opportunity opened when they return and I think the people of Alabama feel that way too," Kennedy said in a twenty-minute speech that was interrupted by applause twenty-five times.

For history has placed us all, Northerner and Southerner, black and white, within a common border and under a common law. All of us, from the wealthiest and most powerful of men, to the weakest and hungriest of children, share one precious possession: the name "American."

Part III

Wednesday, February 14, 1968

Kennedy delivers remarks at the Letcher County Courthouse in Whitesburg, Kentucky, on the morning of February 14, 1968. *Berea College Special Collections and Archives, Berea, Kentucky*

26

8:00 AM—Whitesburg

KENNEDY'S FIRST STOP on the second and final day of his whirlwind tour of eastern Kentucky was the Letcher County Courthouse in Whitesburg. The courthouse had opened just three years earlier, in 1965, but was already considered an eyesore. The boxy three-story building was wrapped in three horizontal bands of blue (some said purple) and white square panels—what one critic later described as "a rare combination of unattractive materials and uninspired design." Jim Webb, a local poet and raconteur, simply called it "the ugliest courthouse in the world." It was also poorly constructed. The roof leaked, and water would drip into the third-floor jail. Inmates would make their displeasure known by clogging their toilets, sending effluent dripping into the offices on the floors below.*

Whitesburg was famous as the home of Harry Caudill, the author of *Night Comes to the Cumberlands*, and for its weekly newspaper, the *Mountain Eagle*. While most local papers in eastern Kentucky were

---

* The courthouse was designed by a Louisville architect named William Banton Moore, who was later involved in a podcast-worthy true crime. Late one night in December 1970, just hours after his wife, Louisa, told him she wanted a divorce, she was found dead in a pool of blood on the floor of an upstairs bathroom in their home. William insisted Louisa must have fallen and hit her head, but the coroner ruled the death a homicide. In a sensational trial the following June, Moore was convicted of voluntary manslaughter and sentenced to twenty-one years in prison, but Governor Wendell Ford commuted the sentence in 1975. Moore died in 1997—the same year the Letcher County Courthouse was completely remodeled.

organs of the local political and business establishment, reprinting press releases verbatim, covering local government inoffensively (if at all), and assiduously avoiding all controversy, the *Mountain Eagle* fearlessly tackled the big issues: corruption, poverty, strip mining, health care. The paper was owned by Tom Gish, a Whitesburg native, and his wife, Pat, who hailed from Paris, Kentucky, a small town near Lexington. They met as journalism students at the University of Kentucky and married in 1948, when they were both in their early twenties.

After the couple took over the *Mountain Eagle* in 1957, they changed the paper's motto from "A Friendly Non-Partisan Weekly Newspaper Published Every Thursday" to "It Screams," and applied the principles they'd learned in journalism school to their coverage of local government, demanding transparency and accountability. This approach did not endear them to local politicians, who were accustomed to conducting business free from the constraints of public oversight. "Although the Gishes wished to blend in with the local fiber of the community," wrote William Farley in "A Stubborn Courage," his history of the paper, "their insistence on honest reporting and open government soon put them at odds with the local power structure." The Gishes were ostracized and occasionally threatened with bodily harm. After reporting on police corruption in 1974, the *Mountain Eagle*'s offices were firebombed. The Gishes updated the paper's motto for the next edition: "It Still Screams."

When Pat Gish, who did most of the reporting for the paper, covered the local school board, she was refused a seat and forced to stand, sometimes for hours, even when she was pregnant. One member of the school board—B. F. Wright, a physician who had delivered Tom Gish and owned several businesses in the county—withdrew his advertising from the paper and forbade the district's teachers from purchasing it. (Such attempted boycotts, Tom Gish later recalled, inevitably improved circulation.)

Malfeasance wasn't hard to find in Letcher County. Besides her work on the paper, Pat also worked for the Letcher County Economic Opportunity Committee, a War on Poverty program. One day in May 1966, her boss, a political appointee named Ottis Amburgey, showed up for work so drunk that he fell off his chair and passed out on the floor.

Amburgey was a former county tax assessor and the son-in-law of a prominent local businessman. Two weeks later, at a meeting of anti-poverty workers in Lexington, Amburgey, drunk again, passed out on a couch in the lobby of his motel. When Gish reported Amburgey to the committee for his on-the-job intoxication, she was fired. The committee later voted to let Amburgey keep his job, but also reinstated Gish.

Harry Caudill found kindred spirits in the Gishes. His op-ed pieces and letters to the editor—usually pointed attacks on entrenched local interests—found a welcoming home in the pages of the *Mountain Eagle*.

Under the Gishes' stewardship the *Mountain Eagle* acquired a national reputation and earned a slew of awards. The paper's offices were the first stop for out-of-town reporters who parachuted into the mountains to cover the latest "hillbilly" story. When Homer Bigart went to eastern Kentucky to report on poverty in the autumn of 1963, he stayed at the Gishes' home. The CBS News correspondent Charles Kuralt became a close friend of the Gishes. For many years he sent them a pair of scissors every Christmas because they always seemed to be losing theirs in the layout room. And when Peter Edelman went to eastern Kentucky to plan Robert Kennedy's trip, he called on Tom and Pat.

The Gishes' son Ben remembers the parade of illustrious visitors who came to his boyhood home. "Hell," he tells me, "they'd shut the presses down and take these people round and show 'em places. I mean, they would miss deadlines to be out taking people like Homer Bigart around when they should have been paying attention to business here, really. I'm glad they did it, but they did it at a big cost."

Tom Gish died in 2008, Pat Gish six year later. Ben now runs the *Mountain Eagle*. Like his parents, he majored in journalism at UK, though he tells me he never intended to go into the family business. "I just didn't have anything else to do. When I got out of school I was gonna apply elsewhere, to other jobs, but then some people who had been here before me, some reporters, left so I just filled in the role and stayed."

We spoke in the paper's spartan offices in a converted garage just off Main Street in downtown Whitesburg. When I asked him if the paper was in the same dire straits that most small-town weeklies seem to be these days, he laughed. "We always are in a dire situation just because of the poor economy here," he says. "The community papers haven't been hit like the dailies on the Internet. We've all lost circulation, though. But ours is mostly due to people leaving and dying. A lot of our circulation loss has come from people who moved away from here after World War II to find work, and they kept the paper going for all those years, but they've died off, obviously."

27

A Winter Tan

Roy Crawford was in the tenth grade at Whitesburg High the day Kennedy came to town. Students were allowed to leave school to see the senator speak on the courthouse steps that morning, and as he raced out of the building, Crawford happened to see his history teacher grading papers at his desk in an empty classroom. "Aren't you going to see Bobby?" asked Crawford. "No," the teacher answered. "I wouldn't cross the street to see Robert Kennedy."

Main Street was already crowded with young people when Kennedy's car pulled up. Standing in front of the building, a long wool jacket pulled tight around him in the morning chill, he spoke extemporaneously, as usual, for a few minutes, stressing the importance of education. "I know how well behaved you youngsters are and how smart you are," he said. "Don't forget to continue your education." Noting that Kentucky's voting age was already eighteen—the voting age wouldn't be lowered from twenty-one to eighteen nationwide until the ratification of the Twenty-Sixth Amendment in 1971—Kennedy joked that he was "going to work for a constitutional amendment to get it lowered nationally to nine."

"I don't have any trouble with voters until they get to be 22," he said, "and then they turn into Republicans." As he left the courthouse, Kennedy told the young people, "Don't forget me when you come of voting age. I'm the one who got you out of school today."

Eleven-year-old Ben Gish stood right in front of Kennedy as he delivered his remarks in front of the courthouse that morning, and afterward he shook his hand. "I don't really remember what he said," Gish tells me. "I was more enthralled by the fact that I'd never seen anybody with a suntan around here in the freakin' wintertime. I remember asking my mom about that and she says it's because wealthy people can afford to take vacations in Florida. Explained all that to me."

Inevitably our conversation turns to contemporary politics. Although Donald Trump defeated Hillary Clinton overwhelmingly in Letcher County in 2016 (80 percent to 17 percent), Gish points out that registered Democrats still outnumber registered Republicans in the county by a margin of more than two to one (11,278 to 4,685 in 2018). "Trump did great here," Gish says, "but all of that came out of Hillary running her mouth and not knowing when to shut up on the coal industry. Her famous quote there. She had the opposite of a way with words. But Trump, the people were desperate. He promised to fix the coal industry. Of course he hasn't. That's what that was. He paid attention to them."

The "famous quote" to which Gish refers was uttered by Clinton at a town hall forum in Ashland, Ohio, on March 13, 2016, when she was asked to "make the case to poor whites who live in Tennessee, Mississippi, Alabama, who vote Republican, why they should vote for you based upon economic policies versus voting for a Republican."

Her answer, in full:

> Instead of dividing people the way Donald Trump does, let's reunite around politics that will bring jobs and opportunities to all these underserved poor communities. So, for example, I'm the only candidate who has a policy about how to bring economic opportunity using clean renewable energy as the key into coal country. Because we're going to put a lot of coal miners and coal companies out of business, right, Tim? [US Representative Tim Ryan, an Ohio Democrat, was in the audience.]
>
> And we're going to make it clear that we don't want to forget those people. Those people labored in those mines for generations, losing their health, often losing their lives to turn on our lights and power our factories. Now we've got to move away

from coal and all the other fossil fuels, but I don't want to move away from the people who did the best they could to produce energy that we relied on.

So whether it's coal country or Indian country or poor urban areas, there is a lot of poverty in America. We have gone backwards. We were moving in the right direction. In the '90s more people were lifted out of poverty than any time in recent history.

Because of the terrible economic policies of the Bush administration, President Obama was left with the worst financial crisis since the Great Depression, and people fell back into poverty because they lost jobs, they lost homes, they lost opportunities, and hope.

So I am passionate about this, which is why I have put forward specific plans about how we incentivize more jobs, more investment in poor communities, and put people to work.

It was, at best, an inarticulate response, and was widely interpreted as an insensitive one as well. Undoubtedly, it was a grievous political error. That single line in the middle of her answer—"We're going to put a lot of coal miners and coal companies out of business"—became an albatross around her campaign, an endless source of fodder for her critics, especially Donald Trump, who repeatedly promised to "bring coal back."

"It's not possible for anyone with more than a passing knowledge of Appalachia and the coal industry to listen to those comments without cringing, regardless of one's political affiliation," wrote public historian Elizabeth Catte in *What You Are Getting Wrong About Appalachia*, her critique of the media's fascination with "Trump Country."

> Clinton's remarks about out-of-work miners are a ghastly but honest flub. But her tone—"those people who did the best they could"—and her poor appropriation of the "coal keeps the lights on" slogan are equally problematic. . . . People didn't "do their best" to keep the nation's lights on; they died.

But as Catte points out, Trump's triumph in coal country was less emphatic than it appears. In McDowell County, West Virginia, for example—a county that the *Huffington Post* declared "unambiguously Trump Country"—Trump defeated Clinton 4,614 to 1,429. But Catte notes that voter turnout was historically low. There were 17,508 registered voters in McDowell County, so only 27 percent of the county's registered voters actually cast a ballot for Trump. Much more damaging than Clinton's "coal gaffe," Catte speculates, was the Democratic candidate's position on abortion, as well as voters' general disdain for politicians, which led many in central Appalachia to simply stay home on Election Day.

For her part, Clinton addressed the "coal gaffe" in *What Happened*, her memoir of the 2016 campaign.

> If you listened to the full answer and not just that one garbled sentence pulled out of it, my meaning comes through reasonably well. Coal employment had been going down in Appalachia for decades, stemming from changes in mining technology, competition from lower-sulfur Wyoming coal, and cheaper and cleaner natural gas and renewable energy, and a drop in the global demand for coal.
>
> I was intensely concerned about the impact on families and communities that had depended on coal jobs for generations. That's why I proposed a comprehensive $30 billion plan to help revitalize and diversify the region's economy. But most people never heard that. They heard a snippet that gave the impression that I was looking forward to hurting miners and their families.

28

To Cure Poverty

THE AIM OF THE WAR ON POVERTY, in Lyndon Johnson's words, was "not only to relieve the symptom of poverty, but to cure it, and, above all, to prevent it." The goal was lofty but not unprecedented, for in the earliest days of the republic one of the B-list Founding Fathers proposed the same thing. In a pamphlet entitled *Agrarian Justice*, Thomas Paine proposed the creation of a "National Fund," out of which every person—male and female, rich and poor—reaching the age of twenty-one would be given a lump-sum payment of fifteen pounds sterling (very roughly $2,000 today), and every person reaching the age of fifty would be given ten pounds sterling ($1,300) annually for life. The scheme would be funded by a tax on property "at the moment that property is passing by the death of one person to the possession of another." An inheritance tax, in other words.

What Paine was proposing was a massive redistribution of wealth from the landed to the landless. It was, in essence, an antipoverty scheme, as well as an early proposal for a guaranteed income. To his fellow founders—especially the "gentlemen planters" Washington and Jefferson, whose landholdings were extensive—it was pure heresy, too revolutionary for the revolutionaries.

Paine himself was an unlikely revolutionary. He was born in Thetford, a market town in the English countryside, in 1737. He moved to London at nineteen but suffered a series of business and personal setbacks that left him, at age thirty-seven in 1774, unemployed, broke, and alone.

Then a friend introduced him to Benjamin Franklin, who was representing American colonies in London. The two became friends, and Franklin urged Paine to start a new life in the New World. Paine didn't need much convincing. "I happened when a schoolboy to pick up a pleasing natural history of Virginia," Paine later wrote, "and my inclination from that day of seeing the western side of the Atlantic never left me."

Clutching a letter of introduction from Franklin, Paine arrived in Philadelphia in December 1774. In less than two years he would inspire a world-changing revolution. Like most immigrants, he quickly adopted local customs and attitudes, and he soon came to consider himself a Pennsylvanian—and an American.

He befriended a printer who hired him to edit a new monthly magazine called the *Pennsylvania Magazine*. Words poured from his quill like water over the falls. Writing under a variety of pseudonyms—Justice and Humanity, Humanus, A Lover of Peace—he published articles attacking a string of injustices: hereditary titles, slavery, "popish principles," pacifism, legalized dueling, and "the horrid cruelties exercised by Britain."

Paine's work caught the eye of Benjamin Rush, a Philadelphia physician, politician, and revolutionary, who urged him to make the case for American independence in a pamphlet. Pamphlets were the eighteenth-century equivalent of tweets without a character limit: cheap to make and easy to disseminate. Small enough to fit in a pocket, affordable even to the working class, and brief enough to be read aloud in public spaces like taverns and churches, pamphlets fueled the era's political and religious debates. Paine originally called the pamphlet *Plain Truth*, but Rush persuaded him to change the title to *Common Sense*. The first edition was published in January 1776. In clear, caustic prose, Paine denounced British "tyranny" and proposed the creation of a new nation in North America, one that would "form the noblest, purest constitution on the face of the earth."

At a time when it was estimated that only about a third of all colonists supported independence, *Common Sense* was a stirring call to arms.

"We have it in our power to begin the world over again," Paine wrote. By the end of 1776 as many as 250,000 copies had been sold, at a time when the population of the colonies was only around three million. Per capita, it is still the bestselling publication in US history.

After a string of military defeats in the summer and fall of 1776, the colonists' enthusiasm for the Revolution began to wane. To shore up support, Paine released a new pamphlet titled *The Crisis*. "These are the times that try men's souls," Paine wrote, turning a phrase that has become epochal.

> The summer soldier and the sunshine patriot will, in this crisis, shrink from the service of their country; but he that stands by it now, deserves the love and thanks of man and woman. Tyranny, like hell, is not easily conquered; yet we have this consolation with us, that the harder the conflict, the more glorious the triumph.

After the Revolution, Paine took up a new cause: deism.

"I believe in one God, and no more; and I hope for happiness beyond this life," he wrote in *The Age of Reason*, a pamphlet published in three parts beginning in 1794. "I believe in the equality of man; and I believe that religious duties consist in doing justice, loving mercy, and endeavouring to make our fellow-creatures happy."

As a deist, Paine did not believe in a supernatural god who interacted with the natural world; the divinity of Christ; or the possibility of miracles. "In every point of view in which those things called miracles can be placed and considered, the reality of them is improbable and their existence unnecessary," he wrote. "They would not . . . answer any useful purpose, even if they were true; for it is more difficult to obtain belief to a miracle, than to a principle evidently moral without any miracle."

The Age of Reason was another bestseller, but the backlash was swift and severe. Critics denounced Paine as a heretic or, worse, an atheist. "Mr. Paine is not an old man, but his faculties are evidently impaired, or he could never have called his book the 'Age of Reason,'" Noah Webster's newspaper, the *American Minerva*, wrote just weeks after the pamphlet was released. *Age* triggered a pamphlet war, a precursor of the Internet flame wars of this century. Dozens of pamphlets rebutting Paine were published. The most famous was *An Apology for the Bible* by a Cambridge professor and Anglican bishop named Richard Watson.

"I begin with your preface," Watson wrote.

> You therein state—that you long had an intention of publishing your thoughts upon religion, but that you had originally reserved it to a later period in life.—I hope there is no want of charity in saying, that it would have been fortunate for the christian world, had your life been terminated before you had fulfilled your intention. In accomplishing your purpose you . . . have thereby contributed to the introduction of the public insecurity, and of the private unhappiness, usually and almost necessarily accompanying a state of corrupted morals.

Watson did not oppose the natural sciences. In fact, he taught chemistry at Cambridge. But his belief in the literal truth of the Bible was unshakable. His argument, in a nutshell, was that the Gospels must be true precisely because the tales the authors told were so incredible: "Had they been imposters, they would have written with more caution and art, have obviated every cavil, and avoided every appearance of contradiction. This they have not done; and this I consider as a proof of their honesty and veracity." Besides, Watson reasoned, the fact that "thousands of learned and impartial men" believed the Bible to be the inerrant Word of God proved that it was. Fifty million Elvis fans can't be wrong.

Thomas Paine responded to Richard Watson in 1797 with his last great pamphlet, *Agrarian Justice*. Instead of rebutting the arguments Watson made in *An Apology*, however, Paine chose to attack Watson's most famous sermon: "The Wisdom and Goodness of GOD, in Having Made Both Rich and Poor." Originally delivered in April 1785, the sermon was subsequently published in a pamphlet (of course) that proved quite popular. Based on his interpretation of Proverbs 22:2 ("The rich and poor meet together: the LORD *is* the maker of them all"), Watson asserted that

God gave the earth to be a means of support to the whole human race; and we have all of us a right to be maintained by what it produces: but he never meaned that the idle should live upon the labour of the industrious, or that the flagitious should eat the bread of the righteous: he hath therefore permitted a state of property to be everywhere introduced; that the industrious might enjoy the rewards of their diligence; and that those who would not work, might feel the punishment of their laziness.

With *Agrarian Justice*, Paine not only rebutted Watson's argument; he rejected its very premise. "It is wrong to say God made rich and poor," Paine argued. "He made only male and female; and he gave them the earth for their inheritance."

There are two kinds of property. Firstly, natural property, or that which comes to us from the Creator of the universe,—such as the earth, air, water. Secondly, artificial or acquired property,— the invention of men. In the latter equality is impossible; for to distribute it equally it would be necessary that all should have contributed in the same proportion, which can never be the case; and this being the case, every individual would hold on to his own property, as his right share. Equality of natural property is the subject of this little essay. Every individual in the world is born therein with legitimate claims on a certain kind of property, or its equivalent.

Since it was impossible to distribute property equally, Paine reasoned, property owners owed a debt to those who owned no property— what Paine called a "ground rent." Hence his National Fund scheme to tax inherited property to provide lump-sum payments to all men and women upon reaching the age of twenty-one, and annual payments to all men and women who achieved the age of fifty.

Paine's proposal is particularly relevant to Appalachia. Consider the following excerpt from *Agrarian Justice*:

It is a position not to be controverted that the earth, in its natural, uncultivated state was, and ever would have continued to be, *the*

common property of the human race [emphasis in original]. In
that state every man would have been born to property. He would
have been a joint life proprietor with the rest in the property of
the soil, and in all its natural productions, vegetable and animal.

Every proprietor, therefore, of cultivated lands, owes to
the community a *ground-rent* (for I know of no better term to
express the idea) for the land which he holds; and it is from
this ground-rent that the fund proposed in this plan is to issue.

Replace "cultivated lands" with "mined lands" and Paine sounds
much like Robert Kennedy speaking 173 years later in Kentucky, when he
called for absentee landowners to pay their fair share of local taxes: "The
outsiders have come in and taken the great wealth that existed in Eastern
Kentucky, and destroyed some of the natural resources, which have not
[been] utilized to the benefit of the people of Eastern Kentucky, and have
created tremendous profits for people elsewhere in the United States."

There is an underlying fury in all of Paine's major works, but it
burns most brightly in *Agrarian Justice*. Paine was always an outsider.
Unlike the vast majority of the other Founding Fathers, he was never
wealthy, never a major landowner, and never owned slaves. He was
sensitive to the plight of the landless, who were denied the right to
vote: "The right of suffrage . . . belong[s] to all equally, because . . . all
individuals have legitimate birthrights in a certain species of property."

Paine believed the National Fund was the only way to address poverty. Private charity was insufficient, he wrote, because "it ought not to
be left to the choice of detached individuals whether they will do justice
or not." Government intervention was necessary.

While the reaction to *Age* had been fury, the reaction to *Agrarian
Justice* was indifference. Paine's proposal was simply too radical to be
taken seriously. By the time the pamphlet was published, the Constitution had been in effect for a decade, and President Washington had
peacefully transferred power to his successor, John Adams. The Republic
was expanding. Vermont and Kentucky had joined the Union. It was no
time to rock the boat. Thomas Paine always rocked boats.

Paine lived his last years in obscurity, poverty, and pain. Bedridden
with gout, he died in the Greenwich Village home of a friend on June 8,

1809. "I am unacquainted with his age," read an obituary in the *Connecticut Courant* signed "Citizen," "but he had lived long, done some good, and much harm." No church would accept his body, so he was buried on a small farm in New Rochelle, some twelve miles outside New York. Just six friends, among them two African Americans, attended the brief graveside service.

Ten years later, in 1819, a British politician named William Cobbett dug up Paine's remains and shipped them to London, where he planned to erect a grand memorial to the great American revolutionary in Trafalgar Square. Unsurprisingly, this memorial to a man that many Brits still considered a traitor never materialized. Cobbett stored Paine's remains in his house. After he died in 1837, they were lost. The final resting place of the man whom John Adams called the father of the American Revolution is unknown.

The War on Poverty renewed interest in Paine's National Fund proposal. In 1966 the economist and futurist Robert Theobald edited a collection of essays published as *The Guaranteed Income: Next Step in Economic Evolution?* "A guaranteed income provides the individual with the ability to do what he personally feels to be important," wrote Theobald. "This will allow risk-taking and innovation in areas where the existing and emerging needs of society are not being met by an otherwise efficiently functioning free-enterprise system."

One of the essays in the book, "The Advance of Cybernation: 1965–1985" by Robert H. Davis, predicted that computer automation— "cybernation"—would result in "the displacement of large numbers of people by machines" in the coming decades. "If we cannot furnish work in the traditional sense for everyone," Davis wrote, "then we will have to find other ways to provide the unemployed with the resources they need to live."* One way to provide those resources: a guaranteed income.

---

* In his essay, Davis, a Michigan State psychology professor who also worked for the Defense Department's Advanced Research Projects Agency, warned that "cybernation" would lead to a loss of privacy: "Often we know little about one another, not because the

"The gross national product of the United States is now about $650 billion per annum," wrote Edward E. Schwartz in an essay titled "An End to the Means Test." "If the federally guaranteed minimum income for a family of four were set at the $5000 per annum modest-but-adequate level the *gross cost* would be less than 7 per cent of the gross national product—still quite tolerable."

In another essay, psychologist and philosopher Erich Fromm extolled the psychological advantages to a guaranteed income.

> A guaranteed income, which becomes possible in the era of economic abundance, could for the first time free man from the threat of starvation, and thus make him truly free and independent from any economic threat. Nobody would have to accept conditions of work merely because he otherwise would be afraid of starving; a talented or ambitious man or woman could learn new skills to prepare himself or herself for a different kind of occupation. A woman could leave her husband, an adolescent his family. People would learn to be no longer afraid, if they do not have to fear hunger.

In 1967 Martin Luther King Jr. came out in favor of a guaranteed income. "I am now convinced that the simplest approach will prove to be the most effective," King wrote in his book *Where Do We Go from Here: Chaos or Community?*

> The solution to poverty is to abolish it directly by a now widely discussed measure: the guaranteed income.
> Earlier in this century this proposal would have been greeted with ridicule and denunciation as destructive of initiative and

---

data is unavailable, but because it is so scattered. There are great pressures to centralize and organize the data because it would greatly facilitate the business of the state. Before the invention of the general-purpose computer, the idea of a central electronic dossier on every individual in the country was impracticable. Today, however, it is technically quite feasible. . . . Under these conditions, the danger to personal privacy is very great. The individual, who has been able to control data about his past and release it at his discretion, will lose this degree of freedom. And since information is power, those who control centralized records will gain enormous power."

responsibility. At that time economic status was considered the measure of the individual's abilities and talents. In the simplistic thinking of that day the absence of worldly goods indicated a want of industrious habits and moral fiber.

We have come a long way in our understanding of human motivation and of the blind operation of our economic system. Now we realize that dislocations in the market operation of our economy and the prevalence of discrimination thrust people into idleness and bind them in constant or frequent unemployment against their will. The poor are less often dismissed from our conscience today by being branded as inferior and incompetent. We also know that no matter how dynamically the economy develops and expands it does not eliminate all poverty.

In February 1968, King announced that a guaranteed income would be one of the demands of the Poor People's March on Washington that spring. In May, more than one thousand economists, including John Kenneth Galbraith, signed an open letter urging Congress to "adopt this year a national system of income guarantees and supplements." Eugene McCarthy, Kennedy's rival for the Democratic presidential nomination that spring, announced his support for a guaranteed national income (and federally subsidized health insurance) in a speech at Boston University on April 11. McCarthy said the federal government should "determine a minimum income which it will assure for all Americans."

Kennedy, however, was skeptical of the scheme. In a speech in Van Nuys, California, on May 15, he said any plan guaranteeing all citizens "a certain income paid for by the federal government . . . simply cannot provide the sense of self-sufficiency, of participation in the life of the community, that is essential for citizens of a democracy." In a thirty-two-hundred-word policy paper released three days later, Kennedy reiterated his opposition to a guaranteed income: "We need jobs, dignified employment at decent pay; the kind of employment that lets a man say to his community, to his family, to the country, to himself, 'I helped to build this country. I am a participant in its great public ventures. I am a man.'" Kennedy said most men prefer work to government handouts. "I myself have met and spoken with these men, white and Negro, from Watts to Eastern Kentucky, from Harlem to Atlanta, and without exception they have said, 'No more welfare. Give us work.'" Dismissing a guaranteed income as "tremendously wasteful," Kennedy asked, "With all the dilapidated housing in America, with the ravaged parklands and inadequate school buildings, with all this work to be done, how can we pay men to sit at home?"

The way to end poverty, Kennedy believed, was jobs—not a guaranteed income from the government. Kennedy's position on the issue put him to the right of McCarthy and appealed to conservative voters. As Daniel P. Moynihan wrote, Kennedy "was now using these views in opposition to another candidate of the left, contrasting his hardheaded, even conservative position with the extravagances of his opponent."

Everywhere he went in eastern Kentucky, Kennedy repeated the mantra: work, not welfare.

29

10:00 AM—Neon,
Waiting for Kennedy

IF THE PREVIOUS DAY'S HEARING at the one-room schoolhouse in
Vortex was unusually casual, the hearing inside the Fleming-Neon
High School gym in Neon was unusually festive.* About one thousand
people packed the forty-year-old gym—"a ramshackle little building
which looks about to slide down the hillside," as one reporter described
it. The school's marching band was there to entertain the crowd waiting
for Kennedy to arrive. The school newspaper, the *Clarion*, printed a
special edition, thanking the senator for coming and for "caring about
the people of Eastern Kentucky." Since it was Valentine's Day, the
paper also included an article thanking St. Valentine for "running the
snakes out of Ireland," a touching if erroneous homage to Kennedy's
ancestral home.

   Waiting for Kennedy outside the gym was a group of about twenty
high school students wearing brown-paper grocery bags on their heads
with eyeholes cut out. Most of the students were members of an activist
youth group based in the town of Evarts in neighboring Harlan County.
The youth group was founded by the Appalachian Volunteers, a War

---

* In 1977 Neon merged with the neighboring town of Fleming to create the present town
called Fleming-Neon.

High school students protesting outside Fleming-Neon High School in Neon, Kentucky, February 14, 1968. *Berea College Special Collections and Archives, Berea, Kentucky*

on Poverty program that began as an informal group of college students who spent their summer vacations volunteering in eastern Kentucky and soon evolved into a full-blown government agency with an annual budget of nearly $1 million.

Around a quarter to nine the Kennedy caravan reached the high school, a two-story redbrick building that sat high up on a hill overlooking downtown Neon. Kennedy went inside and had a light breakfast in the home economics classroom. Around nine fifteen he stepped back outside to mingle with the crowd and noticed the students with bags on their heads standing in a line. They were hard to ignore. On each bag was written a different phrase: ANGRY! ANGRY! or No EDUCATION, No JOBS, No FUTURE or EDUCATION AND POLITICS DON'T MIX. Kennedy, obviously bemused, walked slowly down the line, reading the slogans on each bag quietly to himself. The students themselves didn't say a word. They held a large banner that read, DON'T GIVE PROMISES! GIVE US EDUCATION, JOB-TRAINING.

The students were handing out copies of a newsletter they'd published. Kennedy took a copy and went back inside the school. About forty-five minutes later, just as the hearing was about to begin, one of his aides came out and invited the students inside the gym to get warm.

30

Nell

THE GYMNASIUM WAS PACKED with students "ranging from runny-nosed first graders to high school seniors thinking of leaving the mountains," according to the UPI reporter John Guiniven.

Fifteen-year-old Nell Meade was in the bleachers, along with her fourteen-year-old sister Judy and their thirteen-year-old friend Shirley Gibson. What Nell remembers most vividly about that February day is just how hot it was inside the gym. The temperature outside hovered around freezing, but the boiler room was underneath the bleachers, and the boilers were running full blast. Burning coal, of course. Inside the packed gymnasium it was so hot that, for years afterward, Nell would remember the event as having taken place in August, not in the middle of winter.

Nell's father, Oliver Winfield Meade, who was known by the nickname Odd, was a coal miner. Like most fathers in that place at that time, however, he did much more than mine coal to make ends meet: he also logged, ran a small sawmill, and owned a small auto repair business, which he ran out of his garage. It wasn't easy raising eighteen kids. Nell was number sixteen, and the first of the eighteen to be born in a hospital. The family lived on Kings Creek along KY 160, about twelve miles outside Whitesburg.

Odd instilled in Nell an interest in politics at a young age. "He went four years to school, but he learned a lot and he was a very intelligent man," Nell says. "My father was a very politically thinking man. He understood the value of participating in politics, and he wanted to make sure his children understood that. He wanted to make sure we valued our opportunity to cast a vote, that that was one of the most significant things about being a citizen, to vote.

"He was a Lincoln Republican. His family were totally for the Union. So that was one of the reasons he supported the Republican Party, the party of Lincoln. [Like Mary Rice Farris, Odd was born less than fifty years after the Civil War.] But he voted both Democrat and Republican in local elections. He made it a point to know the people who were running for offices, so he would vote depending on the person who would do the best job. It was always about which one was going to do the best job.

"He was always encouraging everybody to get involved in politics. The day we turned eighteen was the day he took you to get you registered to vote. And we did. And he ran for office a couple times. Didn't get elected. He didn't have any money and even then it was hard to get elected without money. He ran for magistrate. But he was involved with the politics of the county."

When he heard Kennedy was coming to Letcher County to hold a Senate hearing, Odd all but insisted that Nell and her sister attend. "Everybody wanted to go," Nell says. "Everybody knew Bobby Kennedy was coming to town. And we wanted to see that and be a part of that."

It was an exciting day. Odd took the day off work, an extraordinary event in itself. He drove the three girls to Whitesburg to see Kennedy at the courthouse, but they couldn't get very close because traffic was backed up. Nell, Judy, and Shirley got out of the car to walk into town, only to see the Kennedy caravan speed past them on the way to Neon. But even that was exciting. Shirley picked up an apple core that was lying in the road after the cars disappeared down the road. She insisted she'd seen Kennedy throw it out the window of his car. "Now I honestly do not believe Bobby Kennedy threw an apple core out the window," Nell says, "but I think she found it and thought he did, so she cherishes it still."

Odd and the girls then drove to Neon, where he dropped them off at the high school. "Dad waited outside in the car," Nell says. "He was still a good Republican. He wasn't going to get caught hanging out with the Democrats just because he wanted his children to know about Senate hearings."

Nell found herself utterly enthralled by the hearing of the Senate Subcommittee on Employment, Manpower, and Poverty that took place in that dingy old high school gym. And, like so many young people, she fell under Bobby Kennedy's spell. "He was a fantastic speaker and totally knew how to make people understand what he wanted to share with them," she recalls. "And he was easy to listen to—even for me being fifteen and young."

31

Make Yourselves Comfortable

KENNEDY SAT BEHIND A LARGE WOODEN TABLE positioned in the foul lane at one end of the basketball court. Next to him but a bit farther back from the table sat Congressman Perkins. Opposite them was another large table for witnesses. Spectators sat in folding chairs on the floor and in the bleachers on both sides of the court. Sunlight streamed through the windows above the bleachers, near the roof of the gym.

At ten o'clock, Kennedy opened the hearing.

> This visit has a special meaning to me because of the great interest that President Kennedy took in this area, and the fact that he had intended to come here in December of 1963. Now that I'm here and meeting and talking to you, and observing this beautiful land—all this marvelous potential—my visit has even greater meaning. This is a proud land and the mountaineers are proud people, and rightfully so, but I need not tell you that hard times have come to this land, and the people that live in this area; that much of the land has been ravaged by the extraction of its rich resources; the creeks and the streams which run through nearly every hollow are polluted with trash and sewage and acid waste which seeps down from the scarred hills above; wrecked cars

dot the landscape, and the men of our hills who worked at great peril to themselves and their health, and their very lives—these men, many of them who have been disabled by accident and affliction—have been left without work and without hope by the automation of an industry which no longer needed them. Riches still flow from these hills, but they do not benefit the vast majority of those who live here, and I think that situation is intolerable.

The students with bags over their heads were standing in the back of the gym. Kennedy invited them to take seats near the front and "make yourselves comfortable." The official transcript of the hearing notes, "A group of people, wearing paper bags on their heads, comes forward. They are carrying a banner which says, 'Give us jobs and education. We can't eat your fancy promises.'"

Kennedy at the hearing in the Fleming-Neon High School gymnasium, Neon, Kentucky, February 14, 1968. *Berea College Special Collections and Archives, Berea, Kentucky*

32

A Worm in a Miniskirt

TWENTY-ONE WITNESSES WOULD TESTIFY over the next three hours in the stuffy gymnasium. They painted a grim picture of mountain life. "Today the poorest people and the most prosperous corporations in the United States are found right here in eastern Kentucky," Harry Caudill, the first to testify, told Kennedy.

Of the thirty poorest counties in America twenty of them are in eastern Kentucky. Nearly 24% of the white adults over the age of 24 are functional illiterates. A quarter of a million east Kentuckians are expected to leave the region between 1960 and 1970. In some counties more than 25% of the people are on public assistance. In the southern coal fields some 70,000 men are totally disabled as a result of silicosis and pneumoconiosis. The rate of unemployment is higher than anywhere else in America. The region is kept alive by a combination of public works, public medical aids, food stamps, and a multiplicity of monthly checks from the Veterans Administration, the Social Security Agency, and the Department of Economic Security in Frankfort. Only a minority of the people live by direct employment in the region's one major industry—coal mining.

But while the mountains are teeming with poor and under-privileged people, they also bristle with some of the biggest and most prosperous names in America. Within thirty miles of where we sit today there are operations owned by subsidiaries of Ford Motor Company, International Harvester, United States Steel Corporation, Bethlehem Steel Corporation and Republic Steel Corporation. In this county, and in Perry County where you saw the strip mine operations yesterday, are Kentucky River Coal Corporation and Penn-Virginia Corporation. These two companies are, almost certainly, the most prosperous investor-owned corporations in the United States. Last year each of them cleared more than 61% of gross receipts after the payment of all taxes and operating expenses and paid dividends equal to, or in excess of, 45% of gross receipts. Thus their dividend rate was nine times as high as that paid by Standard Oil of New Jersey and General Motors.

Only Appalachia and the great oil fields of Texas are rich enough to support such wealthy concerns.

Caudill excoriated "the vast absentee interests which . . . had assumed complete control over the region's economic and political destiny," and he urged Kennedy to propose legislation imposing a federal severance tax on "all minerals extracted from the earth anywhere in the United States." And he helpfully suggested the rate: 5 percent of the gross sale price of the mineral.

When Caudill finished, Kennedy thanked him effusively. "That was a very excellent statement, Mr. Caudill," the senator said, "and very, very helpful to the committee." Sitting in the audience, watching Caudill and Kennedy commend each other, was a Bethlehem Steel executive named Dave Zegeer, and he was fuming.

Gussie Vaughn, a mother of nine, begged Kennedy to make the school lunch program free for all students. (The cost had recently risen from five dollars a month to thirty cents a day.) Cy Hamilton, who described himself as "an old retired miner," said there was "lots of hunger" in eastern Kentucky.

We was in a place here not long ago—I hate to tell you this—it was a girl, she is about seven or eight year old, a big snow on the ground, barefooted and no shoes to wear to school. The Appalachians [the Appalachian Volunteers] got out and fixed her up some shoes, and got her some food to eat so the girl could go to school. I thank you now. I thank you for being here. But I would druther all these government programs, we would all work together and not work again[st] one another but all work together. That's my sentiments.

Hamilton also told Kennedy that jobs were disappearing because machines were replacing men in the mines. "In '60 we was running 244 ton of coal a day with 144 men," Hamilton explained. "They moved this machinery in. You know what they done. They run 325 ton of coal there with 22 men. That was all the hitch. It took all the work away from us."

Doane Fischer, a Harlan County pediatrician, told Kennedy that "far too many children in our area are getting a diet that is both qualitatively and quantitatively inadequate." Fischer said a survey of 109 children attending Harlan County preschools found 50 percent of the children had intestinal parasites and 60 percent had severe tooth decay.

During a brief break in the proceedings, a man rose from his seat and approached Kennedy. "Could I speak just a word?" he asked Kennedy. "Since you came down here from Washington to talk to the poor people of Eastern Kentucky, and me being one of the poorest and one of the—I've got the largest family in Letcher County—and I draw more food stamps than anybody in Letcher County. Since I'm the poorest, I believe you should let me speak just a word."

Kennedy agreed to let the man testify. His name was Cliston Johnson, though everybody knew him as Clickbird. An unemployed father of fifteen, Johnson was born and raised in Partridge, Letcher County. At Kennedy's urging, he took a seat at the witness table and unfolded a piece of paper on which he had typed a statement.

Although we are in the center of the United States here in the mountains of Eastern Kentucky, we are isolated from the rest of the world, and, although we are some of the proudest people in the world, we have always been the laughing stock of the rest of the nation. We are the target of television, the movies, books, and newspapers, and downgraded as the most ignorant and unlearned people in the world. This is not true by a hell of a long shot. True, we are poverty-stricken people, but not sorry as some may believe. We are only in poverty because our political leaders have sold us down the river and because we have had no worthwhile representation.

Most of our leaders live in the Blue Grass and are not interested in the mountain people after election time. I appreciate the efforts of President Johnson and the few Congressmen and Senators who try to help us poor people, but so far, they have hardly reached the poor man. Ninety-nine percent of the money appropriated for poverty in Eastern Kentucky is spent before it reaches us. Office workers and other well educated men and women draw large salaries, and the poor man gets the crumbs that fall from their tables. The poor man has to stand in line for hours hoping to get a measly little handout. He is as much out of place in their air-conditioned offices as a worm in a miniskirt. And when someone is cut off a government program, it's always the poor man. . . .

All we poor people want is to be able to help ourselves. We need a worthwhile program where the poor people can have a job and work for a living. We don't want to depend on the government all our lives. It seems to me that we are being held in the poverty line intentionally. For instance, if you live in a housing project, and you make a little extra money, they raise the price of your food stamps. . . . What we need is a work program for all poor people—handled directly by the government or by the poor people themselves. This would eliminate all politicians and all men who have become richer from the money appropriated for poverty-stricken people.

I thank you.

Senator Kennedy responded, "That was worth waiting for, Mr. Johnson."

Johnson told Kennedy that his income was $60 a month, out of which he paid $26 for $112 in food stamps. That left him just $34 a month for all other expenses, including rent, utilities, "and a hundred other things."

"I'm not able to work," Johnson explained, "but I get out and do what little bit I can—trade and traffic around. It's not easy. These food stamps last this family only about two weeks, and from that on it's beans and bread and the next week it's bread and beans."

The audience laughed knowingly. Kennedy, however, was incredulous. "You support fifteen people in your family on the $112.00 [in

Cliston Johnson testifying at the hearing at Fleming-Neon High School.
Berea College Special Collections and Archives, Berea, Kentucky

food stamps] a month?" he asked. Johnson confirmed that he did but
added that he also hunted for food. "I mean like it was back in the old
mountaineer days, you know, we catch what we eat."

"You ought to come to my house sometime and see them fifteen kids
in the bed," Johnson said. "Did you ever see fifteen kids in three beds?"

"I'm moving in that direction," Kennedy replied.

"The more children you've got," Johnson advised Kennedy, "you
just add a little more water to the gravy."

Seated at a table set up in the foul lane of the basketball court, Congressman Carl Perkins (left) and Kennedy listen to Cliston Johnson's testimony. *Berea College Special Collections and Archives, Berea, Kentucky*

33

The AVs

IN LATE JANUARY 1964, less than a month after Lyndon Johnson announced
the War on Poverty in his State of the Union address, the Council of
the Southern Mountains, a nonprofit group founded in 1912 to promote
development in Appalachia, convened the first meeting of the Appalachian Volunteers at the CSM's headquarters in Berea, Kentucky. Milton
Ogle, the thirty-year-old director of the CSM, had recruited a handful of
students from Berea College to repair tumbledown schoolhouses in eastern Kentucky the following summer. They would be joined by students
attending the other colleges in that part of the state, including Pikeville
College, Alice Lloyd College, and Eastern Kentucky State College.

In the summer of 1965 the number of student volunteers grew to
150, including some from outside the state, and their mission expanded
beyond school repairs. An AV report noted:

> They built roads and bridges, tilled land, repaired community
> buildings, and sat down with local people to worry about prob-
> lems of sanitation in homes without plumbing; sewage disposal
> in communities without municipal services; preventive medicine
> in areas largely without doctors; legal aid for people who can-
> not afford lawyers. These were the earliest days of the "war on
> poverty," and Appalachian Volunteers were its earliest troops
> in Eastern Kentucky.

When he was in law school, Steve Cawood volunteered for the AVs. He trained other law school students who came from out of state to volunteer between semesters. "We had this fleet of pickup trucks," he remembers, "and we had kids that'd never driven. They came out of New York or Boston or someplace and they'd never driven. We'd have to teach them how to drive. And then we'd have to teach them how to drive in eastern Kentucky, on a gravel road. Shit, they'd get those damn trucks stuck or run 'em in the creek or hit things, tear 'em up, so we had trouble keeping insurance on them."

Cawood also helped the volunteers find a place to stay, usually in the homes of local families happy for the extra income—about five dollars a week. Then he'd teach them how to navigate the complex local bureaucracy for clients entitled to government benefits such as Social Security, food stamps, and welfare payments. The eligibility standards were much more stringent back then, Cawood says, and the process could be cumbersome and time consuming, involving lots of paperwork. Many clients were illiterate.

"There was one case that was just unbelievable," Cawood recalls. "One of the kids came in and said, 'I got a fella in Knox County that can't get his old-age Social Security benefits because he doesn't have a driver's license.' He couldn't prove his age. And these people were flabbergasted. And that was as shocking to me as it was to them. I couldn't imagine that that was the case. But he had been delivered by midwives. What mountain people call granny women.

"His name was Sam Brown. He's now dead. Sam was born on Stinking Creek. And we proved his case with affidavits and depositions from six or eight women who were present when he was delivered. He had worked all his life just at odd jobs and little small coal mines where there were no records kept. Working in the log woods, cutting timber, where there were no records kept. Small lumber mills. And just kind of help people with their tobacco crop or help people around their farm. Just subsistence living. And he had never had a paycheck where he had had Social Security deducted."

It took years—the case went all the way to the US Court of Appeals for the Sixth Circuit in Cincinnati—but Sam Brown eventually got his benefits.

In 1966 the Appalachian Volunteers broke away from the Council of the Southern Mountains, and Milton Ogle became the now-independent organization's director. The AVs operated in fourteen counties in eastern Kentucky with more than three hundred volunteers, including many from VISTA, and a paid staff of thirty-four, twenty-three of whom were local people. "Thus," wrote Ogle in a letter to Kentucky governor Edward Breathitt defending the program in October 1967, "the organization is, as it has always been, a combination of local people and 'outsiders'—something that can be and is overlooked from time to time among charges of 'outside agitation.'"

Inevitably this combination sometimes led to conflict. "Some of these Volunteers are from way outside, and you can tell," one mountaineer told an OEO program evaluator in 1966. "They have a different tempo. They expect things to happen—fast, right before your eyes. It's not so much that they're impatient; it's that they expect their impatience to *work*, so that when they try to do something, it'll get done overnight. But we have long overnights here."

The list of the organization's accomplishments is long. Indeed, judged purely by the quantity of projects the Appalachian Volunteers undertook, the organization must be considered one of the most ambitious government programs in American history. The AVs built community centers; organized woodworking workshops and sewing circles; set up job-training programs in mechanics and other trades and helped unemployed miners find work outside the mines; taught families how to better manage their finances; opened health clinics, libraries, and thrift shops; started preschool programs, including Head Start (itself a War on Poverty program), summer schools and community newsletters in remote hollows, and summer schools for youth with mental disabilities, a group that many school districts at the time simply ignored; organized youth baseball and softball leagues; distributed clothing and vitamins to needy children and organized a "Bread Buying Club" to purchase day-old bread from local grocers and distribute it to needy families; held pie suppers and quilt raffles to raise money for local programs and helped market handicrafts—like quilts, jewelry, and chess and checker sets— outside Appalachia (a handmade quilt that fetched five dollars in eastern

Kentucky might command fifty dollars in New York); helped repair water systems and dirt roads; collected trash, cut weeds, and cleared creek beds; and even started a taxi co-op to serve residents in counties where public transportation was nonexistent.

The Appalachian Volunteers may have been too successful for their own good.

Some local officials took umbrage with the implication that their communities were somehow deficient. An AV named Judy Stewart tried to start a hot lunch program at the Darby Branch School, a one-room school in Clay County. Stewart helped Verelee Sizemore, a mother of nine whose children attended the school, pitch the idea to the other parents. "I'm new at this here community action the A.V.'s talk about," Sizemore told her neighbors. "[It] means people like us taking a hand in trying to solve problems that plague us. I say one of them problems is our kids don't get no dinner at school. How about us pitching together to see what we can do?" All the parents agreed, but when Sizemore approached the teacher with the idea, the teacher said, "These kids don't want no lunch at school." Then Sizemore went to the school superintendent, Mallie Bledsoe, to solicit her support. "Mrs. Bledsoe seemed to consider the whole project a reflection of the inadequacies of 'her' school system," Judy Stewart wrote in a memo to Milton Ogle.

> She refused to let the group put the necessary equipment in the school. She said schools in Clay County didn't need "outsiders" bringing things in; she provided the schools in the county with "basic necessities" and . . . certainly would not agree to let the mothers fix the food and concluded the interview by saying that the school and the community should be regarded as two separate things. It was all right for parents and A.V.'s to be involved in community projects but *she* ran the school and would appreciate it if there was no further interference [emphasis in original].

The vast majority of the funding for the AVs came directly from the federal government through the Office of Economic Opportunity. In 1966, for example, the OEO provided 98 percent of the organization's $883,000 budget. This posed an existential threat to local politicians in eastern Kentucky, who were accustomed to federal funding being funneled through their offices.

Given the times, it was perhaps inevitable that the Appalachian Volunteers came to be involved in protest movements. Most conspicuously—and controversially—the AVs organized protests against strip mining.

The Appalachian Volunteers also established four "education outposts" in eastern Kentucky, including one in Evarts, Harlan County. Each of these outposts was staffed by one full-time AV employee who was responsible for "conducting workshops in welfare rights, community organization, health programs, and child care." In 1967 the AV in charge of the Evarts outpost was a twenty-four-year-old woman from Gary, Indiana, named Jeanette Zimek.

Zimek had come to Harlan County three years earlier, arriving on a Trailways bus late one night in September 1964, having chosen to forego her senior year at the University of Chicago to volunteer in Appalachia. Her father, a Czech immigrant named Vaclav "James" Zimek, died five months before she was born. He was on his way to work at the Union Carbide plant in Whiting, Indiana, one morning in January 1943 when the car he was riding in was hit by a New York Central train at a grade crossing in East Chicago. Widowed, with a two-year-old daughter and another child on the way, Jeanette's mother, Margaret, received a $7,000 settlement from the railroad. Margaret later remarried, though her second husband, Jeanette remembered, "did not bring love or affection into the household, and I think my mother always regretted the marriage."

In 1961 Zimek enrolled at Chicago but found herself much more interested in activism than academics. She joined the Quaker Student Fellowship, and in the summer of 1963 worked on the Fort Berthold Indian Reservation in North Dakota as part of a Quaker program. The following summer she worked on another Quaker project with migrant workers in Delaware.

In the summer of 1964, unhappy at college, Zimek decided to apply for a two-year Quaker work program. She was accepted and assigned to work as a community development worker in Harlan County. Living in a hollow called Jones Creek, Zimek helped build a kitchen in the community's one-room schoolhouse and distributed food and clothing to needy families. When that program ended, she was hired by the Appalachian Volunteers and moved to Evarts, a town of twelve hundred wedged into a deep valley on the Clover Fork of the Cumberland River.

34

The *Cloverfork* *Newsletter*

ONE OF THE GOALS OF THE AVs was to work with young people, to moti-vate them to get involved in their communities, and to offer them oppor-tunities for recreation, socializing, and entertainment. The entertainment opportunities for young people in eastern Kentucky fifty years ago were meager: high school sports and extracurricular activities, a movie, cruising. Even if your family could afford a television set, the viewing options were limited. So, working out of a rented house in downtown Evarts, Jeanette Zimek set to work organizing a youth program for students attending Evarts High School. (A few students from two other Harlan County high schools, Cawood and Cumberland, also joined the group.)

Many of the youth groups that the AVs established were affiliated with traditional organizations: 4-H, Girl Scouts, Boy Scouts. But some sprang from the grass roots, unencumbered by the constraints of insti-tutionalized organizations and free to pursue their own agendas. Such was the case with the Cloverfork Youth Group in Evarts, which, wrote historian Jessica Wilkerson in *To Live Here, You Have to Fight: How Women Led Appalachian Movements for Social Justice*, "spoke out about daily injustices and offered keen critiques of the systems of power in Harlan County, drawing on the language of the civil rights, student, and free speech movements."

The club brought together a small, interracial group of students who, as one of the former students recalled, were all misfits and not part of the in-crowd at the high school. Students in the group were outspoken, and some of them challenged heterosexual norms—one female student was an avowed tomboy, and several of the young men eventually came out as gay. They also tested racial boundaries; before the youth group officially began, Jeanette had helped to arrange an interracial swim party at an all-white swimming pool in Harlan County. As a group they showed an interest in how the civil rights movement rippled through Harlan County. They also challenged adults and students alike to analyze the roots of poverty in eastern Kentucky.

The twenty to thirty students in the Cloverfork Youth Group met once or twice a week at the outpost in Evarts to "discuss social issues and their own particular problems." They were continuing Harlan County's long tradition of radical politics, stretching back to the Mine Wars of the early 1930s. "We were considered almost like communists," one member of the group, Peter King, recalled in an oral history interview recorded in 2015 for the Berea College archives. "And they"—his teachers—"actually thought the Appalachian Volunteers were communists and that they were there to disrupt our little town instead of helping. And the only thing they wanted to do was help."

Peter King was born in 1952 and grew up "in a little holler called Pounding Mill." His father was a disabled coal miner and a veteran of the First and Second World Wars. His mother was a homemaker. Peter had nine siblings, though he says the family wasn't poor, at least compared to his neighbors. Through his disability payments and his veteran's benefits, along with whatever work he could find on the side, his father provided for the family sufficiently if not extravagantly.

Peter was eleven when his school, Black Mountain Elementary, was integrated.

The first time black kids came to Black Mountain, I'll never forget that day. The white parents had guns. And here comes walking up this little hill Luther, Winston Carr, Janice Carr,

Jackie Kennedy—there was like six or seven black kids coming up. And these little faces come up—and this is what you have guns for? You're afraid of this? And after that day it was OK. And we were all friends. I didn't understand prejudice. Because everybody seemed to get along.

By the time he was five, Peter already knew he wanted to get out of Harlan County. "I used to think, *Why am I here? Why am I not in New York City? Or Chicago?*" The Cloverfork Youth Group offered him a way out. "The Appalachian Volunteers helped all of us realize there's more things in the world than just this little town. This little town's cute—but it's not necessarily where we wanna be the rest of our lives. We don't have to stay here. We can go somewhere else. We can go help people somewhere else," he said. "The first trips I ever went on outside of Harlan County were with the Appalachian Volunteers." He would move to Louisville after high school and wouldn't return to Harlan County for thirty years. (His sister, on the other hand, was perfectly happy there and didn't set foot outside the county until she was seventy.)

"Everybody was afraid to join it," King recalled of the youth group. "People would just laugh at us like we were bad. We were trying to help people. We were trying to help each other. The teachers—everybody—I don't remember one person being for us. We were almost ostracized for what we had done."

Peter recalled how the youth group pressured the school to offer a course in black history—or negro history, as it was known at the time.

> They fought us tooth and nail to keep that class from coming. We had to have eight people in the class and we got 'em so we were allowed to have that class. We were going against the school board and the school teachers and making a school teacher teach a class he didn't want. But it was a law that said if you had eight students that want that class, it had to be offered. And our youth group, we made that happen. And we got a teacher that hated us. He seemed to really not like us because he had to teach this class. We were just studying on our own. He just didn't care.

(The teacher was white.)

In the autumn of 1967, the youth group began publishing a newsletter. The bulk of the *Cloverfork Newsletter* comprised reports cataloging the unsatisfactory conditions at Evarts High School. Opened in 1937, the two-story brick building in downtown Evarts was dilapidated and overcrowded. Some classes were held in rickety "temporary" trailers parked behind the school. Brenda Bailey (now Brenda Bailey Taylor) joined the group soon after it started. She was sixteen and in the eleventh grade. "Oh, it was nasty," she says of the high school. "The girls' bathroom was nasty. There was never no tissue paper in there and there was one cracked-up mirror. One of the first things we started writing about in the newsletter was about trying to get funds to get the school fixed. But the school board took it personal and got pissed off. They said, 'You're writing subversive material about your high school.'"

"This group decided that the most important thing to them was getting a decent building to go to school in," recalled Jeanette Zimek (now Jeanette Zimek Knowles). "It was suggested to them that if this was so important to them, why didn't they do something about it?" In the third issue of the newsletter, dated January 22, 1968, the students published an editorial explaining their mission.

> The purpose is to bring forth the facts, to carefully weigh and consider them. The purpose is to print the truth, to aro[u]se the interest in our students. The purpose is to let the parents know of the conditions their children must endure while securing their education: the unsanitary conditions of the washrooms—such as, no paper, no soap, faucets that do not work, the smell, commodes that overrun. Some of the outside buildings are—face it or not—fire hazards. There isn't a school in Southeastern Kentucky with nineteen buildings with three public roads intervening with each student walking around ½ mile a day. What inspiration could a student have in a building with the floors not having been cleaned in two weeks, desks not having been cleaned during the school year, and clothes being torn by barbed wire, loose screws in doors, etc.?
>
> This newsletter will deliver the truth; it will deliver the facts to the students and others regardless of our personal sacrifices.

CLOVERFORK NEWSLETTER

Issue 4   MARCH 21, 1968   Volume 1

SENATOR ROBERT KENNEDY INSPECTING BAGS AT HEARING

The March 21, 1968, edition of the *Cloverfork Newsletter*, the first published after Kennedy's visit. *Jeanette Zimek Knowles*

So go on, give us detention hall, suspend us if you will. Our determination will not waver, but become even stronger.

Just like the striking coal miners who fought the mine operators and private deputies three decades before, only to be starved back to work, the Cloverfork Youth Group learned there would be repercussions to their activism, a price to pay—even if they were still just teenagers attending a public high school. "I was a really good student," Peter King recalled.

> And when we started working with the Appalachian Volunteers and fighting to get things we wanted, everything went downhill from there. I started getting bad grades—even though I'd made good grades. When my report card would come out instead of saying an A it would say C. [The teachers] did that all the time. I was actually being called a communist. They called my parents and told them I was involved with communists.
>
> The counselors that were supposed to be there to help us, when we were in this youth group, they never helped us. There was no help to try to get me into college or anything like that. They would just totally ignore us. There was nothing we could do about it.
>
> They didn't want us to mess with anything. They didn't want us to fight the school board. People would laugh at us. I actually got bullied all the time because of it. I'd get punched and pushed all the time. It didn't stop us though. We wanted change. We wanted to do something for the school.

The students' parents had mixed feelings about their children's participation in the youth group. "A few of the parents took up for 'em," Brenda Bailey Taylor tells me, "and a few of the parents didn't took up for the students, so you pretty much had to take care of yourself."

Through the fall of 1967 and into the winter, the *Cloverfork Newsletter* published photographs chronicling the high school's deficiencies: a crumbling bathroom ceiling, piles of garbage behind the school, sewage leaking through a hole in a brick wall. There were little things too. Letters on the building's facade spelled out EVARTS HIGH SCHOOL, but the

S in SCHOOL was missing—and had been for three years, according to the newsletter. Most of these incriminating photographs were taken by the Cloverfork Youth Group's undisputed leader, a stocky, blond-haired kid who never, ever backed down from a fight: Tommy Duff.

35

The Average Homosexual

THOMAS CLAUDE DUFF WAS BORN in Evarts on October 1, 1949. His father, Thomas Duff Sr., was a coal miner. Tommy's mother, Ova, was a homemaker. His friends recall that both parents drank too much and that Tommy's father may have been physically abusive to both Tommy and Ova.

"He had a rough life," his friend and fellow member of the Cloverfork Youth Group Thelma Parker (now Thelma Witt) tells me. "He was friendly and outgoing, but there were home problems." Like his parents, Tommy had a drinking problem, and Witt remembers visiting him in jail one time after he was arrested for public intoxication.

"He was a genius," Brenda Bailey Taylor remembers. "But he had a very hard home life. But his daddy worked. That's one thing I can say. He worked hard. When you look in the yearbooks, he [Tommy] had a suit on in his pictures, and when you'd see him in the hallway, he had good clothes."

"Tommy Duff was very outspoken," Jeanette Zimek Knowles, the Appalachian Volunteer in charge of the Cloverfork Youth Group tells me. "Kind of a rascal, one might say, who saw the humor in things and could crack a joke." But he had a temper too. "Tommy Duff was so involved and so angry," Peter King recalled of his friend. "And he was smart too. People picked on him all the time. He was very vocal. But he was big enough to fight. He wouldn't back down from anything."

Tommy Duff's senior picture in the 1967–68 Evarts High School yearbook. *Brenda Bailey Taylor*

Tommy was five eleven, 206 pounds, according to his draft records. He helped design and lay out each issue of the *Cloverfork Newsletter*, and at Christmastime he would earn a few extra dollars by painting holiday scenes on the windows of shops in downtown Evarts. "He was a great artist," Brenda Bailey Taylor says. He was also a member of the high school chorus and the debate club.

Tommy was gay, and though he wasn't out, he didn't go to great lengths to hide the fact either. "He had a friend, and the way they were with each other, you just picked it up," Thelma Witt recalls. Still, growing up gay can be difficult even under the best circumstances, and growing up gay in the mountains of eastern Kentucky in the mid-to-late 1960s was especially difficult.

For a 1995 article in the *Journal of the Appalachian Studies Association*, sociologists Kate Black and Marc A. Rhorer interviewed five lesbians and four gay men from central Appalachia, ranging from twenty to forty-five years of age. (Tommy would have turned forty-six in 1995.)

The researchers "found several common themes in the rich stories of the participants: feelings of isolation, the importance of community, fears from inside and outside the closet, various forms of oppression and discrimination, and identity."

The feelings of isolation in the mountains were especially acute: "While growing up, participants said, they had no one to turn to for guidance, support, and information when they began realizing they were homosexual. People felt there were no others with same-sex attractions, even to the extreme that some did not know gays or lesbians existed." Two of Tommy's classmates in the Cloverfork Youth Group later came out as gay, but it's possible that none of the three was aware that the others were gay. As one gay man told the researchers of his high school classmates whom he later discovered were also gay, "At the time I thought they were people I got along well with, but I didn't realize why. . . . I didn't know people who were gay."

"The saddest part to me about growing up in the mountains as a gay person is that . . . you end up feeling like an outsider," a lesbian whom the researchers interviewed said. "You've got no one to talk to about these strange feelings you have and you have to end up like lots of young people growing up gay, being isolated, and you think about killing yourself 'cause you're so strange."

On March 7, 1967, when Tommy was seventeen, the *CBS Reports* program aired a documentary called "The Homosexuals." Hosted by future *60 Minutes* correspondent Mike Wallace, the program did not depict homosexuals in a positive light. "The average homosexual, if there be such, is promiscuous," Wallace declared gravely in the broadcast. "He is not interested or capable of a lasting relationship like that of a heterosexual marriage. His sex life, his love life, consists of a series of one-chance encounters at the clubs and bars he inhabits. And even on the streets of the city—the pick-up, the one-night stand, these are characteristics of the homosexual relationship." (Years later, Wallace would say he regretted the program's clear antigay bias.) Although some affiliates refused to carry the program, it still garnered huge ratings. If Tommy happened to see it that night, it probably didn't make him feel very good about himself.

36

Paper Bags

WHEN IT WAS ANNOUNCED that Kennedy would be holding a hearing at Fleming-Neon High School, just fifty miles east of Evarts on US 119, the students in the Cloverfork Youth Group were excited. "We all loved the Kennedys," Peter King said. "We knew what they were doing. They were for the poor people. They were rich people for the poor people. They didn't have to be in politics. Never had to. They were always wealthy. They just wanted to help people."

The youth group also saw Kennedy's visit as an opportunity to express themselves on a grand scale. In the spirit of the times, they wanted to make a statement, to stage a zap. And they were in a combative mood. On February 5, Evarts High School principal O. G. Roaden suspended Tommy Duff indefinitely, allegedly because he'd been caught taking pictures of conditions inside the school. In an article published in the *Cloverfork Newsletter* after the Kennedy hearing, the students explained why they went to Neon.

> We went there to try the best way we knew how to get a better educational system. We know this will take a long time, but perhaps we can get a new school building in the meantime. Sure, we are going to get a gym extension of about twenty feet and several new classrooms, but by the time this happens, we will be out of school. You may say, "Then why worry about it?" For

one thing, we might have children who will have to go to the same dump that we have to go to. You may say that it was good enough for you and it should be good enough for us. I think that when people think like this, they have a very dull outlook on life. If you try with us, I think we can get a better school and educational system.

Nobody remembers who came up with the paper bag idea, but the message the students wanted to send was clear: they felt voiceless. Their schools were inadequate, their futures uncertain. And nobody was listening to them. The youth group explained why they wore the bags over their heads in an article published in the *Cloverfork Newsletter* after the hearing.

> A great number of people can't seem to see the reason why these students presented themselves to Robert Kennedy in such a manner. Some people are under the impression these students were ashamed of themselves or scared.
>
> These students did have reasons for wearing bags over their heads, but fear or pride was not among them. Their reasons are as follows.
>
> 1. You're in a bag when you graduate from school in Harlan County. When you graduate from High School in Harlan County, you are in a bag that isn't easy to get out of. Whether you go to college or get a job, you will see where you have been cheated.
> 2. These students would not have been seen or heard anyway. Kentucky was allowed only one spokesman of school age. This spokesman was to have an allotted amount of time to speak. What can be said about educational problems that exist all over a state in two to seven minutes? Since these students weren't *really* going to be seen or heard, why shouldn't they cover up their faces and their mouths? Also, since they wouldn't have a chance to say what they wanted those people to know, they wrote it on their bags and signs.
> 3. To draw attention. If these students hadn't worn bags over their heads, they would have been just a bunch of kids

in the back of the room. No one would have known they
were there or that they had a problem.

The youth group published a special edition of the newsletter to
hand out at the hearing. It included more photos of the school and an
editorial by Tommy Duff that was highly critical of school administra-
tors. The students met in Harlan at six o'clock on the morning of the
hearing and carpooled to Neon.

Peter King recalled how it felt to wear the brown paper bag: "I'm
kind of claustrophobic, so it wasn't a good moment, with a bag over my
head!" When they walked into the gym, King remembered, the crowd
went completely silent.

When Kennedy asked which of the students would like to testify, there
was no doubt who it would be. Tommy Duff took the bag off his head
and slid into the chair behind the big wooden table set up across from
Kennedy, who was holding the special edition of the *Cloverfork Newsletter* the youth group was handing out that day. Kennedy asked Tommy
to read the editorial he'd written for the special edition. Tommy obliged.

Last week I was expelled from Evarts High School for taking
pictures. I was taking pictures of wash rooms with fallen plaster,
students standing around a potbellied stove, students crossing
road intersections to get to class, converted commissaries and
shower rooms for classes, and other deplorable school conditions.
To my knowledge there has never been a regulation restricting
picture taking on school premises. But the fact is, somebody
doesn't like it. Perhaps it's what the pictures will be used for.

For the past two and a half months I have been working
with a group of students from Evarts High School who have been
printing a publication called the *Cloverfork Newsletter*. In this
newsletter there have been articles on washrooms with no soap,
paper, or heat, poor heating in much of the school, broken desks,
falling intercoms, coal dust from the tipple, no fire escapes, and
crowded school buses. There have also been articles on freedom

of speech and press, Evarts residents sending their children to other schools, where school funds come from and how much money is spent on education in Harlan County, teacher salaries in the county compared to state and national average salaries, and profit made on coal and timber in the county.

Some of the pictures which I took will be included in our next newsletter. Perhaps they will explain more clearly what we are talking about. But apparently somebody is afraid to have these pictures circulated—afraid of having the truth revealed.

The Principal who expelled me threatened to turn my name in to the draft board if I didn't agree to stop working on the Newsletter, but if I did agree to stop what I was doing, he could probably get me on the NYC program. [The Neighborhood Youth Corps was a youth employment program.]

Should I take this offer of a job or should I continue working for what I believe in—better education?

If I do continue to fight for better education, will you fight with me?

"I didn't come here today to burn my draft card," Tommy added. "I came here to protest but not to protest against the war in Vietnam. I came here to protest about one thing. . . . When you graduate from a [high] school in Harlan County you have just about the same education as a person that graduates from the eighth grade."

Tommy's remarks were met with sustained applause. "We left feeling that we accomplished what we came for," the youth group wrote in the next edition of the newsletter. "Young people were noticed. We were recognized as *people* of Appalachia who now have a voice."

The day after the hearing, Evarts High School principal O. G. Roaden said Tommy's testimony was "about as false as you can make"—a rather serious accusation to lob at a witness testifying before a Senate subcommittee. "He was suspended until his father and mother would come in and be responsible for him," Roaden told the *Harlan Daily Enterprise.* "The suspension was for other disciplinary reasons (than taking pictures) and he has been suspended several times before." He also claimed Tommy took the photographs in question after, not before, he was suspended. According to the principal, "At the time the pictures

Kennedy listening to testimony at Fleming-Neon High School. *Berea College Special Collections and Archives, Berea, Kentucky*

were taken . . . a teacher reported that Duff was accompanied by a 'long-bearded' person who was driving a Jeep with Kenton County license plates." (Kenton County is an urban county just across the Ohio River from Cincinnati.)

The youth group fired back at Roaden in the next edition of the newsletter, publishing an unsigned letter from one of Tommy's classmates.

> On February 5 I was sitting in my fourth period class when Tommy Duff came into the room to work on his science project. He had the pictures that he had taken that morning of the very bad conditions of the school. Tommy was called to the office, so he asked me to keep the pictures until he saw me again. I kept the pictures until I saw Tommy at lunch when he told me that he was suspended from school for taking the pictures.

The letter was accompanied by a petition signed by twenty-seven students who also said they saw the pictures before Tommy was suspended.

Obviously, I was eager to find Tommy Duff and interview him for the book. A cursory Internet search quickly revealed, however, that he had died in Los Angeles on May 25, 1971, just a little more than three years after his encounter with Robert Kennedy. Curious about his fate, I ordered a copy of Tommy's death certificate from the California Department of Public Health. It arrived about three weeks later. It said Tommy died of "multiple stab wounds to [the] abdomen."

The official cause of death was listed as suicide.

37

The War on Welfare Queens

THE WAR ON POVERTY SET what today seems an outrageously ambitious goal: the federal government—working with state and local governments, private enterprise, and community organizations—would eradicate poverty in the United States. End it. Wipe it out. But, coming just thirty years after the depths of the Great Depression, and on the heels of total victory in a global war and the resulting economic boom, it seemed, for a time, an attainable goal. Certainly, many Americans thought, the world's richest country should be able to eradicate poverty—unlike the godless hellholes of China and the Soviet Union, where famine had claimed millions earlier in the century. Similar to the space race, eradicating poverty was another way to prove American superiority.

Ultimately, of course, the War on Poverty did not end poverty as we know it in America. But it came closer than most people realize. From 1959 to 1973, the official poverty rate was cut in half: from 22 percent to 11 percent. On a chart, the steady downward trend is unmistakable. Poverty in the United States seemed headed for extinction. But then it stopped declining, and since 1973 it has stubbornly remained between 11 and 15 percent.

What happened? For one thing, unlike the Cold War and the space race, support for the War on Poverty was not bipartisan. Republican opposition was philosophical (it was not government's role), practical (it was too expensive), political (it was a ruse to promote civil rights), and, ultimately, cynical: if the War on Poverty succeeded, liberalism would benefit at the expense of conservatism. Conservatives were terrified. Another major Democratic interventionist adventure—the second in the century after the New Deal—was proving successful. So they worked to undermine it.

The end of the War on Poverty—and the end of poverty's decline—coincided with the rise of conservative Republicanism in the 1970s, culminating with the election of former California governor Ronald Reagan as president in 1980.

While conservatives fought antipoverty initiatives legislatively—including conservative Southern Democrats, ten of whom joined twenty-two Republicans in voting against the Economic Opportunity Act of 1964—they also fought them in the court of public opinion. It was Reagan himself who hit upon the most successful anti-antipoverty trope: the so-called welfare queen.

Reports of welfare fraud are as old as welfare itself. A *Louisville Courier-Journal* investigation found widespread welfare fraud in the city—in 1885. "In my connection with the work, which lasted about eighteen months, I did not find a single case of a street beggar that was worthy," the former director of one charitable organization told the paper. "Some fifty cases were investigated, and all of them turned out to be fraudulent in some sense."

With the Great Depression came more reports of welfare fraud. In July 1930 a forty-seven-year-old Detroit man named Peter Turkiela was arrested for illegally obtaining twenty-four dollars from the city's welfare department after he admitted that he had "$700 in the bank, owned two lots and recently bought the home he occupies." Turkiela was sentenced to a year's probation.

Perhaps the earliest use of the term *welfare queen* in the media occurred in 1964, the same year the War on Poverty was launched, when the *San Francisco Examiner* affixed the label to a thirty-five-year-old mother of thirteen from Oakland who had been receiving welfare for fifteen years.

Twelve years later, in 1976, Reagan made the welfare queen a central theme of his unsuccessful campaign to challenge Gerald Ford for the Republican presidential nomination. "In Chicago, they found a woman who holds the record," Reagan said at a campaign rally in January 1976. "She used 80 names, 30 addresses, 15 telephone numbers to collect food stamps, Social Security, veterans' benefits for four nonexistent deceased veteran husbands, as well as welfare. Her tax-free cash income alone has been running $150,000 a year." This anecdote rarely failed to elicit gasps of amazement from his audiences.

Unlike many Reagan anecdotes, however, this one was reality based. A Chicago woman named Linda Taylor was, in fact, suspected of perpetrating a massive scheme to fraudulently obtain welfare payments. The case, however, was hardly typical. Taylor was a sociopath and professional grifter who was also suspected of burglary, insurance fraud, and murder. In fact, most welfare fraud is perpetrated by poor people who use the illicit gains to purchase necessities—like food—not fancy cars. But the meme proved irresistible to right-wing politicians and pundits.

"With her story," Josh Levin wrote in "The Welfare Queen," an article for the online magazine *Slate*,

> Reagan marked millions of America's poorest people as potential scoundrels and fostered the belief that welfare fraud was a nationwide epidemic that needed to be stamped out. This image of grand and rampant welfare fraud allowed Reagan to sell voters on his cuts to public assistance spending. The "welfare queen" became a convenient villain, a woman everyone could hate. She was a lazy black con artist, unashamed of cadging the money that honest folks worked so hard to earn.

While Robert Kennedy and other liberal Democrats had attempted to humanize the poor—by, for example, shining a bright light on them and their plight—conservative Republicans, like Reagan, attempted to demonize them. And it worked. As the popular *New York Times* columnist Russell Baker wrote in 1985, "Welfare queens crystalized public anger about big budgets into public hostility against government programs to help the unemployable classes."

38

Dave Zegeer

DAVE ZEGEER WAS A COMPANY MAN through and through. He loved Beth-lehem Steel, and he loved coal mining, both of which, he believed, were forces for good in eastern Kentucky. So, as he sat in the Fleming-Neon High School gym listening to Harry Caudill "slandering" his company and his industry, Zegeer seethed. Although he realized it was akin to Daniel entering the lion's den, he asked Kennedy for a chance to respond.

Zegeer was born in Charleston, West Virginia, on August 27, 1922. His parents, Assad and Amelia, were Lebanese immigrants, and Dave was the seventh of their eight children. Assad was a candymaker who died when Dave was just four years old, leaving Amelia to raise the chil-dren alone. "We had to make out with what we had," Zegeer recalled. "And we did, under my mother's leadership."

Dave graduated from Charleston High School in 1940 and enrolled in West Virginia University, the only one of his siblings to attend col-lege (and, he later joked, "the only one so stupid he needed college to make a living"). He intended to major in electrical engineering—until he spent a summer working in his brother's grocery store in the West Virginia coal town of Whitesville. "I learned to like everything about the coal people and their way of life," he said. "Everybody was down to earth and friendly. I was actually fascinated by these wonderful people." When he returned to school that fall he changed his major to mining engineering. He graduated in 1944 and, after two years in the army, he went to work for Consolidation Coal Company in Jenkins, Kentucky, as a surveyor.

Over the next eight years, Zegeer steadily rose through the ranks, becoming assistant to the president in 1954. Two years later, Bethlehem Steel bought Consolidation and appointed Zegeer superintendent of its Beth-Elkhorn mining division in eastern Kentucky.

At the time, Bethlehem was one of the largest landowners in eastern Kentucky. Founded in 1904, the company controlled a tangle of subsidiaries that mined the coal that fueled its blast furnaces. Bethlehem made the steel that built the Golden Gate Bridge and the Empire State Building. It was America's biggest shipbuilder and second-biggest steel producer (after US Steel). (Bethlehem Steel went out of business in 2003. A casino now occupies the site of its flagship mill in Bethlehem, Pennsylvania.)

Zegeer earned a reputation as a mine operator who put his workers' safety first. Miners were required to attend weekly safety meetings, and supervisors underwent a lengthy safety training program. Between 1956 and 1976, the number of reported accidents in Beth-Elkhorn mines plunged from about twelve per million man-hours to less than one. Zegeer also promoted gender and racial equality in the mining industry, and he hired the first women in the United States to work as underground coal miners. In 1983 President Reagan would appoint him to oversee the federal Mine Safety and Health Administration, and during his four-year tenure, mine fatalities would fall to record lows.

Inside the Fleming-Neon High School gymnasium, Zegeer took his seat behind the witness table across from Senator Kennedy and Congressman Perkins. "We are quite honored to have you gentlemen here with us," he began, "but I thought it might be well to bring out a few points."

> DAVE ZEGEER: The gist of what has been said is that absentee ownership—whatever that means—that that is bad. I might mention Bethlehem Steel has eight hundred stockholders in the state of Kentucky; they are the stock owners of the corporation.
>
> SENATOR KENNEDY: How many stockholders [overall]?

ZEGEER: In the thousands, sir, I don't know, but I do know there are eight hundred in Kentucky.

KENNEDY: I suppose if there are eight hundred—out of how many? That's the question.

ZEGEER: I would say fifty to seventy-five thousand. I really don't know. [*Laughter*] There are eight hundred here, but I'm not interested in names, primarily. But I do want to leave this with you. Eleven years ago—

KENNEDY [*interposing*]: You would hardly say that was a Kentucky-owned company, would you?

ZEGEER: Well, there is eight hundred stock owners in Kentucky. But eleven years ago Bethlehem bought the operating property here in our area, and the thing I was wanting to impress on you, I was here before Bethlehem came, but Bethlehem coming here was one of the finest things [that] happened to this area. I do wish to leave these figures with you: One is that last year we produced 2,300,000 tons of coal, which left $950,000 in the Mine Workers Welfare and Retirement Fund, to help support the hospitals. In addition to that, we donated $50,000 to these Appalachian Regional Hospitals, and that is one of the important things I think has been done for this area, by putting these hospitals in. In addition to that, the statements were made [that] we pay no tax. That's not right. Last year alone we paid $200,000 in property tax; a total of $500,000 in all taxes. Now altogether in taxes and donations and welfare funds, we poured one million and a half dollars in this area. In addition to that . . . we have about 850 employees in this area, which is about four or five thousand people that are supported by those 850 workers, and these 850 workers earn $6,887,693 or roughly $6,900,000. An average income per worker of about $8,000. We own 7 percent of the surface in Letcher County and pay 20 percent of the taxes . . .

KENNEDY: Again, I think what we try to stress is that we would like to have more industry in this area and not less industry, and that would provide more jobs for all people. I suppose as you look back over the history of eastern Kentucky you would have to reach the conclusion there has been absentee ownership. . . . I'm not from Kentucky, but I can certainly see what has happened here, and I have read the history of Kentucky, and I know that's part of it. Would you agree with that?

ZEGEER: No, I would not, but I don't think we have time to debate all of it. I think, in part, some of your statements are correct, but also the great wealth, as you say, it has been left here and not taken out.

KENNEDY: As I go around, as I did and have, I recognized the great wealth that existed in this state; I recognized the great wealth that has gone out of the state, going to all parts of the rest of this country, and then all around the world, and I see people by the thousands with not enough to eat, and obviously there has not been a proper distribution of that wealth to the people of eastern Kentucky.

ZEGEER: I do thank you for the opportunity to let me give you at least our side of one operating company in the area. We are proud of the area and like the area. You will not find any better group of workers. Frankly, I might end by saying this, that publicly, we are sorry we don't have jobs for everybody here, but we are one company. We are proud of being here; we feel like we are doing a good job, and I wouldn't want you to leave feeling that any operating company was bad.

39

The Zegeer Files

DAVE ZEGEER DIED IN 2012 at age ninety. He had amassed a large collection of mining memorabilia, most of which was donated to a small museum in downtown Jenkins that bears his name. The David A. Zegeer Coal-Railroad Museum occupies a restored train depot and is crammed with vintage mining equipment and tools, as well as photographs, prints, postcards, and ephemera. Dave Zegeer, it turns out, was a pack rat. The walls are covered with hard hats, headlamps, augers, saws, and lunch pails. Hanging on a wall in the back of the museum is a portrait of the man himself in middle age, wearing a dark jacket and tie, smiling slightly, with intense dark eyes and a full head of thick gray hair closely cropped.

I wanted to know more about this man. Steve Cawood, who'd ridden along with Kennedy on his tour and was in the Neon gym when Zegeer testified, suggested I get in touch with Steve Gardner, a mining engineer who was just getting started in the business when he worked for Zegeer at Beth-Elkhorn in the 1970s.

Although he was quite busy—President Trump had nominated him to head the federal Office of Surface Mining Reclamation and Enforcement, and he was in the midst of the byzantine confirmation process—Gardner graciously agreed to meet with me at his firm's office in Lexington. So, on a rainy July morning, I found myself in a conference room whose walls were lined with mining books (*The Blasters' Handbook*) and thick

A portrait of Dave Zegeer hangs in the David A. Zegeer Coal-Railroad Museum in Jenkins, Kentucky, December 2018. *Author's photo*

binders labeled HAZARDOUS WASTE and DRAINAGE. Handsome and affable with Reaganesque hair, Gardner looks like a politician, but he was finding his first foray into high-level Washington politics endlessly frustrating. He'd submitted lengthy financial disclosure statements and had even agreed to surrender his interest in his own consulting firm to satisfy conflict-of-interest requirements, but confirmation by the Senate still seemed a distant dream.*

---

* In September 2018 he finally gave up and withdrew his name from consideration. "The cost and uncertainty just became overwhelming and I decided it was time to get on with life," he wrote in a letter to friends. "So, it is back to work and trying to catch up on some of the lost opportunities from the last year."

Hard hats on display at the David A. Zegeer Coal-Railroad Museum.
Author's photo

Gardner tells me his bachelor's degree was actually in agricultural engineering. (He later earned a master's in mining engineering.) Zegeer hired him right out of college in 1975 to work on mine reclamation projects. By then Zegeer was a legend in the mining industry. "We called him the Godfather," Gardner recalls. "He had a house in Jenkins, and we called it the Ponderosa." As for the Kennedy hearing, Gardner says Zegeer once told him it was a "no-win situation." "Dave was a consummate gentleman," Gardner says. "He never raised his voice. Nobody could say a bad word about him."

Gardner founded his firm, ECSI (Engineers Consultants Scientists International), in 1983. (In January 2019 the firm merged with SynTerra Corporation. The new company is called SynTerra.) Gardner has worked on energy and mining projects throughout Appalachia. Like Zegeer, he is an unapologetic advocate for coal mining. "There is a real 'war on coal' waged by activist groups, agencies and many in the press," Gardner wrote in a 2014 op-ed for the *Lexington Herald-Leader*. "I have seen the combatants and the casualties."

When Dave Zegeer died, his family asked Gardner to help them catalog his papers. "Dave was an organized hoarder," Gardner explains. It seemed Zegeer had kept a file on everything. "Did he keep a file on Robert Kennedy?" I ask hopefully. Gardner gets up and pulls a thick manila folder off a shelf and sets it on the table in front of me. It is labeled KENNEDY, ROBERT. Inside is a cornucopia of news clippings and correspondence, much of it relating to Kennedy's Kentucky trip and the hearing at Fleming-Neon High School.

The folder offers a fascinating glimpse behind the scenes of the public relations battles playing out over strip mining in eastern Kentucky in the late 1960s. On February 19, 1968, six days after the hearing, Zegeer sent a two-and-a-half-page, single-spaced memorandum to Thomas J. Crocker Jr., the vice president of Bethlehem Steel's mining division. "We had reasons to believe that this hearing would be another opportunity for Attorney Harry M. Caudill to put his philosophies before the public and into the Congressional Record and condemn the coal industry in toto while doing so," Zegeer wrote.

> He invariably points the finger at a few companies, including Bethlehem, when he makes his charges that these companies are robbing the area of its wealth, contributing very little in the way of taxes, destroying the land or doing untold damage to the small surface owners. All of these things he attributes to acts by absentee owners, one of whom is Bethlehem. Such absentee landlords, according to Mr. Caudill, extract the coal at tremendous profits and leave behind a ravaged land and the "halt and the lame." And as expected, Mr. Caudill did present a most unfavorable image of the coal industry and Bethlehem Steel.

Zegeer went on to recap his testimony, portraying himself in the most positive light—it was a memo to his boss, after all. "The discomfort of Harry Caudill was very obvious when he learned Mr. Zegeer was to appear before the hearing," Zegeer wrote in the third person. "It was also quite apparent that Mr. Caudill supplied the questions that Senator Kennedy asked."

"[Caudill] singled out Bethlehem and a few more large companies and such statements, allowed to go unchallenged, undermine all of the efforts of Bethlehem's Public Relations programs and efforts," Zegeer wrote in a cover letter attached to the memo. "It is our feeling that every effort should be made to counteract the adverse publicity Mr. Caudill is giving the coal industry in general and Bethlehem in particular."

Obviously, Dave Zegeer and Harry Caudill were adversaries. Nonetheless, they maintained a cordial, even friendly relationship over the years. Buried in the Zegeer files was an article about the Kennedy hearing that appeared in the Council of the Southern Mountains' monthly magazine, *Mountain Life & Work*, in January 1970. Caudill had carefully cut the article out and sent it to Zegeer. Still paper-clipped to it was a cheeky note: "DAZ—Thought you might enjoy a reminder of Bobby's visit to Eastern Ky.! Harry."

40

All the Girls

WHEN THE HEARING IN THE GYM ENDED, the Fleming-Neon High School band struck up "Hello, Dolly!" and the students who'd sat patiently in the bleachers throughout the long hearing streamed onto the gym floor and mobbed Kennedy as if he'd just sunk a buzzer beater to win the state championship. "For the girls it was a Valentine's Day dream come true," according to UPI's John Guiniven. "'He's handsomer than Paul Newman,' screamed one teen-ager. 'I'll never wash my hand again, 'cause he shook it.'"

Nell Meade (now Nell Meade Fields) admits she was among the starstruck that day. "It was like seeing one of the Beatles," she says. "More so for people like me that had really strong political urgings. I think people had developed a fondness and a love for that family just because of what they had been through with the loss of the president. And so it was easy to idolize him and care about the Kennedy family. And then Bobby had his own charisma. People were crazy about him. All the girls had a crush on Bobby." Nell, her sister Judy, and their friend Shirley needed an excuse for missing school that day. Judy came up with an idea. She took a piece of scrap paper and wrote on it:

> Please excuse from school
> Nell Meade
> Judy Meade
> Shirley Gibson
> They attended my meeting

Fleming-Neon High School closed in 2005, when it was consolidated with two other Letcher County high schools to create the new Letcher County Central High School in Ermine. The building, shown here in July 2018, is now used as a middle school. The gymnasium where the Kennedy hearing was held was torn down and replaced around 1976. *Author's photo*

"And she took it up and got him to sign it," Fields says. "He signed it. I think it was more of an autograph. He didn't really know what he was doing. But he signed it! And we took it back to school and it worked perfectly. The teachers were very impressed. I still have it in a little frame."

The Cloverfork Youth Group wasn't as lucky. One of Kennedy's aides called Evarts High School to get them excused for the day, but Principal Roaden refused to believe the caller, insisting it was a "damn communist VISTA" impersonating a Kennedy aide. The Evarts students who attended the hearing were suspended for two days for the unexcused absence.

Cynics dismissed the hearing as nothing more than a publicity stunt. "It ain't us he cares about," one man outside the gym told a reporter, "it's them TV cameras and microphones." But Nell Meade, at least, left the hearing elated. "I remember coming away feeling so much better about myself and my lot in life," she says. "I felt a great respect and

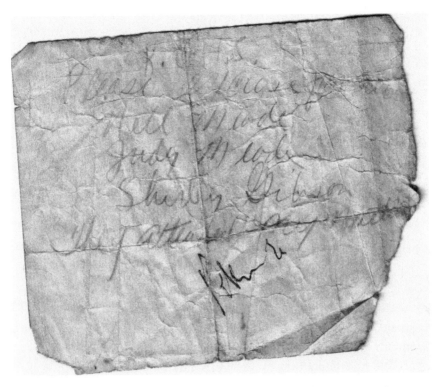

The "permission slip" that Kennedy signed for Nell Meade, Judy Meade, and Shirley Gibson after the hearing at Fleming-Neon High School.
Nell Meade Fields

appreciation for my people and people like me, and how he responded to the people in need. Hearing his responses and his caring nature being shared so openly and honestly, you could feel that he really cared about people. It made me feel better as a person and it gave me great hope. Great hope for my future. It was like having the light put out when President Kennedy was killed and having it put back on again when Bobby came and talked to us about what the future could be."

41

4:00 PM—Prestonsburg

FROM NEON, ROBERT KENNEDY made his way to Prestonsburg. Along the way he stopped to meet with poor families in the hollows of Hemphill and Haymond. He visited Mark B. Smith, his wife, and their six children in Haymond. Mr. Smith told Kennedy his monthly income was just eighty dollars and he could afford to buy fresh milk only once a month. Kennedy asked Mrs. Smith what the family had had for breakfast that day. "Gravy," she said. What about lunch? "Beans." And what would supper be? "Beans again, I guess," Mrs. Smith said "with dejection," according to one report. Mark Smith told Kennedy he was bitter because "if you don't hang in that clique [at the courthouse] in Whitesburg, you don't get nothin'." Congressman Carl Perkins told him, "We'll do all we can." "I wish somebody would," Smith said. "They sure ain't doin' it here."

In Prestonsburg, Kennedy delivered brief remarks at the Floyd County Courthouse. Gary Parr, a VISTA worker attending Prestonsburg Community College at the time, helped prepare the remarks. Although he was a McCarthy supporter, Parr gladly volunteered to help Kennedy's staff arrange the Prestonsburg stop. "They just wanted me to come up with a list of local dignitaries for him to thank," Parr tells me. "But I prosed it out so I could say I wrote a speech for Bobby Kennedy." Parr was wearing a McCarthy button when he met Kennedy, which greatly amused the senator from New York. "Robert Kennedy looked right at me and said, 'But you're supporting Mr. McCarthy,'" Parr remembers.

"He smiled. He knew we would all change to him. McCarthy was about as exciting as a desk drawer."

From a small airport near Prestonsburg, Kennedy flew to Louisville on Governor Louie Nunn's plane. That night he attended a reception in his honor at the home of Mary and Barry Bingham Sr., the publishers of the *Louisville Courier-Journal*. It was a lavish if unbefitting end to his two days in Kentucky.

Kennedy meeting with residents of Haymond, Kentucky, February 14, 1968.
Berea College Special Collections and Archives, Berea, Kentucky

Kennedy chatting with James Johnson in Johnson's home, Hemphill, Kentucky, February 14, 1968. Johnson owned a small store in the town. *Berea College Special Collections and Archives, Berea, Kentucky*

42

From the Kentucky
Coal Mines . . .

AFTER THE KENNEDY HEARING, the Cloverfork Youth Group became decidedly more radical. The students attended the Poor People's March on Washington in June. The group also adopted a new name that summer—the Harlan County Youth Liberation Movement—and changed the name of its newsletter to the *Youth Movement*. The articles in the newsletter became more political and less parochial, addressing issues bigger than the woeful state of Evarts High School: racism, poverty, voting rights, Vietnam.

But funding for the Appalachian Volunteers was drying up. Under intense political pressure—particularly from Kentucky's Republican governor, Louie Nunn—the Office of Economic Opportunity slashed funding for the AVs in 1969 and eliminated it altogether in 1970.

The last issue of the *Youth Movement*—formerly the *Cloverfork Newsletter*—was published on April 14, 1969. Two months later, Jeanette Zimek moved to Oregon for a VISTA job, but she would return to eastern Kentucky in the fall of 1970 to resume her antipoverty work.

By the time the last edition of the newsletter was published, Tommy Duff had left Harlan County for good. His movements in the year or two immediately after he left Evarts are hard to track. His parents and his only sibling, a sister, are all deceased, and his only living relatives seem to be his sister's two children—Tommy's niece and nephew—who were both born after he died. Tommy dropped out of high school just shy of graduating in the spring of 1968. "He left," his friend Brenda Bailey Taylor tells me. "It got too hard on him, and he just couldn't take it anymore."

Tommy may have moved away to avoid the draft. He wasn't a draft dodger, per se; more like a draft avoider. After he dropped out, he lost his student deferment and the Evarts draft board changed his classification to 1-A. He then asked to be reclassified as a conscientious objector, but this request apparently was denied. When the draft lottery was held on December 1, 1969, however, Tommy lucked out. His birthday—October 1—was assigned number 359, virtually guaranteeing he would never be drafted. (Each day of the year was randomly assigned a number, and men were drafted in that order. September 14 was assigned number 1, so all eligible men born on that date were certain to be drafted. The highest number drafted was 195—September 24.)

Friends remember that, like so many young people who left the mountains, Tommy migrated to Indiana to find work. This was a familiar destination for many young émigrés from the mountains. During the Second World War and the decades that followed, Appalachian expats found ample opportunities for employment in the factories and mills of Hoosier boomtowns like Indianapolis (engines), Muncie (auto parts, glass), and Gary (steel). Employers, in turn, prized Appalachians for their presumed indifference to unionism. "Haven't you heard there are only 45 states left in the Union?" *Harper's* magazine "joked" in 1944. "Kentucky and Tennessee have gone to Indiana and Indiana has gone to hell."

Like immigrants from foreign lands, migrants from Appalachia tended to settle together in enclaves where they could keep their customs and cultures intact, such as the Fountain Square neighborhood in Indianapolis. New arrivals could find a warm welcome and familiar faces and connections to economic and cultural opportunities in these Little Appalachias. Also like immigrants from foreign lands, migrants from Appalachia were frequently subjected to wanton discrimination. During the Great Depression, an official in Muncie complained that the city's rising welfare rolls were due to "the cumulating cost of human

debris thrown on the city by the heavy importation of hillbilly labor."
As recently as 2014, the *Muncie Star Press* reported, "Real or perceived
scorn for those with Southern backgrounds remains a periodic source
of tension locally at times, certainly when the 'h-word' is raised."

The Appalachian diaspora, like the exodus of African Americans
from the South, represents one of the great internal migrations in American history. It also represents a tragic loss of human industry, intellect,
and ingenuity in the mountains. The exodus has ebbed and flowed over
the decades, fluctuating with the fortunes of the coal industry. But the
overall trend since the end of the Second World War is unmistakable:
those with the means and the inclination to leave, leave. Between 1950
and 1970, the population of Harlan County fell 48 percent (from 71,751
to 37,370). It rebounded a bit in the 1970s, due to a mini coal boom
created by the Arab oil embargo, but in the 1980s it resumed its downward trend. Between 2010 and 2016, the population of Harlan County
fell 7.2 percent, and the populations of the six counties that border it
fell by between 4.8 and 7.1 percent each. The estimated population of
Harlan County in 2016 was 27,168.

The same scenario has played out in counties throughout eastern
Kentucky and indeed all of central Appalachia. Faced with limited economic and social opportunities and alienated from the local power structure, Tommy Duff faced the same difficult decision many young people
in eastern Kentucky—especially members of the LGBTQ community—
still face today: stay or go. Tommy went, but efforts are underway to
convince more young people to stay.

STAY, in fact, is the name of an organization founded in 2008 by
young residents of central Appalachia. Officially known as the STAY
Together Appalachian Youth Project, the group describes itself as "a
network of young people, aged 14–30, who are committed to supporting
one another to make Appalachia a place we can and want to STAY."

"A lot of the folks who formed it were queer," STAY's project coordinator Lou Murrey tells me. "But it's not queer-focused, it's much
broader. We want to fight the notion that you have to leave, or that
the only opportunity is if you leave. We're also a network for people
who leave and want to come back."

"What makes it more tolerable to stay in a region is if you have a network of people or you have a community," she says. "So creating community—people who you can fall back on—people who will be there for you. I know I can go anywhere in Appalachia and have a place to stay. Anyplace, because there are STAY members there that I'm connected to. So, in very tangible ways and in not-so-tangible ways, it's creating a support network."

Murrey says jobs are part of the solution to out-migration—but only a part. "We can have jobs, but what are those jobs gonna be? Are they gonna be the same extractive jobs that put us in this position we're in? Do we want more coal mining jobs except a little cleaner? We want jobs that don't break our bodies and our spirits. We want jobs that pay us a living wage. There are jobs in Appalachia. There's jobs at the grocery store, jobs at the Dollar General, jobs at the Walmart. It's just that they don't pay us enough to survive.

"When we talk about jobs programs, usually they're not very good. Usually it's a call center. A call center is coming into Danville, Virginia, for a payday loan company." The company, PRA Group, buys "bad debts" from lenders, including payday loan companies, and tries to collect payments from the debtors. "Payday loans ruin people's lives. . . . We're not going to be building our communities on the backs of other people's suffering. That's not what gets us to freedom. That's just perpetuating a cycle that has not done us any favors. They call it progress, but progress for who? How many of these jobs are going to provide health insurance? Any economic development that doesn't take into account how good the jobs are is bad economic development."

Murrey also tells me she dislikes the term *brain drain*. "It implies that the people that choose to stay—the young people who are here—are not smart," she says. "That what's left are the dregs. And it implies that young people are a resource to be extracted. It commodifies young people's lives."

When he was in eastern Kentucky, Robert Kennedy spoke of the need for young people to stay in the region:

> Riches still flow from these hills, but they do not benefit the vast majority of those who live here, and I think that situation is intolerable. So the best of your young men who are educated and

trained are forced to leave eastern Kentucky and go off to other parts of the nation to search for work, and the old, the sick and weary and those who know no other life, who have been the coal miners who have made this part of the land; who contributed their strength and their sweat and their skill and their courage to making this part of the country—they are left behind.

Tommy Duff was in the audience at Fleming-Neon High School when Kennedy spoke those words. If STAY had existed fifty years ago, Tommy Duff might've never left Evarts. But it didn't, and he did, and sometime in the spring of 1970, he made his way west, to that mecca of all young dreamers, Hollywood.

43

... to the California Sun

IT'S NOT KNOWN WHY TOMMY chose to move to Los Angeles. Perhaps, like countless young people before him, he was attracted to the glitz and glamor. Perhaps he harbored fantasies of stardom. Or maybe he was just eager to come out and live openly as a gay man. In any event, Tommy created a new life for himself in Los Angeles. He told his new friends that he'd played football for the University of Kentucky and that he dated a girl in college until he met her brother and "turned homo."

While less conspicuously flamboyant than its counterpart up the coast in San Francisco, the gay scene in Los Angeles in the early 1970s was no less vibrant—despite constant harassment from the Los Angeles Police Department, which was notorious for sending undercover cops into gay bars to "conduct surveillance" and arrest patrons for lewd behavior.

One such raid took place on New Year's Eve 1966 at the Black Cat tavern, a popular gay bar on Sunset Boulevard in the Silver Lake neighborhood. A few minutes after midnight on January 1, 1967, while a band played "Auld Lang Syne" and same-sex couples exchanged celebratory kisses, twelve plainclothes officers from the LAPD vice squad began beating patrons to the ground with their fists and guns. "They did not identify themselves except by their weapons," according to a press release issued soon after the incident by the Tavern Guild, a consortium of gay-bar owners in California. The police arrested at least fourteen people, some of whom were badly beaten.

Outraged by the Black Cat raid, a small group of gay rights activists who called themselves Personal Rights in Defense and Education—PRIDE—organized a rally on the sidewalk in front of the tavern on the evening of February 11. Dozens of people turned out, marching silently with homemade signs reading NO MORE ABUSE OF OUR RIGHTS AND DIGNITY and BLUE FASCISM MUST GO! The protesters were careful to follow the letter of the law, marching in silence, for fear of being arrested for disturbing the peace, and never standing still, for fear of being arrested for loitering. It was a quiet and subdued affair. Yet it was historic, because, occurring more than two years before the more famous Stonewall riots in New York, it was one of the first organized gay-rights demonstrations in American history.

But attitudes were not easily changed. Later that same month, a group of homeowners in the Pacific Palisades neighborhood complained to the LAPD about three local bars that were "frequented by a homosexual element." The police were sympathetic. "It is a case of a better class wanting undesirables out," Captain Sidney S. Barth explained to the *Los Angeles Times*. "We can't arrest a man because he's a homosexual. We can arrest him if he commits a homosexual act, but only then. Similarly, we can't arrest a man because he has a beard or because he's a beatnik."

Although the atmosphere was often hostile, gay culture flourished in Los Angeles, and the milieu in which Tommy Duff found himself was probably unlike anything he'd ever imagined—much less encountered—back in Evarts: gay pride parades, gay-ins, a gay community services center and legal aid society, a gay hiking club and bowling league, a gay thrift store (Gaywill Funky Shoppe), even a gay church (Metropolitan Community Church). There was a gay newspaper, the Los Angeles *Advocate*, which later morphed into a glossy monthly magazine with a nationwide circulation. And, of course, there were the gay bars—at least eighty—strung along Sunset and Santa Monica Boulevards and tucked into the neighborhoods of Echo Park, Silver Lake, and Hollywood, each offering seemingly endless opportunities for entertainment and hooking up.

It was liberating and at times surreal. It was also overwhelming, and, as he had in high school, Tommy often found refuge in the bottle. On one occasion he was arrested after he was found passed out on the street.

Tommy was also arrested for prostitution. He was a sex worker. When a friend asked him why he did it, Tommy replied that he "didn't want to work at a regular job" because he "needed a great deal of money." Despite—or perhaps because of—his humble upbringing, Tommy had expensive tastes: a nice apartment, nice clothes.

Tommy managed to keep in touch with a few old friends in Evarts. Thelma Witt remembers getting a call from him one day. He told her he'd met Rock Hudson at a party. Tommy told his friends back home that he was working in a grocery store. (On his death certificate his occupation was listed as "Clerk, Super Market.")

In March 1971, when he was twenty-one, Tommy started dating a recently returned Vietnam veteran named Walter Yeargin Jr., who went by the nickname Doug. Yeargin was only a year older than Tommy but had already lived an adventurous life, to say the least. Born and raised in South Bend, Indiana, the son of a tool-and-die maker and a homemaker, Doug did not grow up in a happy home. His parents fought constantly, usually about money.

Doug joined the Marine Corps right out of high school in 1967. He was trained as a medic and sent to Vietnam. Shortly after he arrived, Doug's platoon was conducting a sweep near a village called Đà Sơn when it was ambushed by North Vietnamese troops. The platoon suffered heavy casualties, according to an account published in his divisional newspaper, the *Southern Cross*:

> Although wounded himself, Yeargin continued to expose himself to the enemy fire while traveling from man to man administering first aid. In an attempt to get near the wounded men a medevac copter was shot down a short distance from the pinned down platoon; Yeargin again exposed himself to the enemy to reach the downed craft where he helped evacuate the crew and administer first aid to its injured members.

For his heroism he was awarded the Silver Star, the military's third-highest honor for valor. He later received the Bronze Star after a helicopter he was riding in was shot down in a remote area and he administered first aid to his injured crewmates. Specialist Yeargin was honorably discharged after three years of service. He'd come out as gay while he was in the Marines and wanted to live openly as a gay man. In January 1971, Doug moved to Los Angeles. Two months later, he met Tommy Duff.*

Tommy and Doug rented an apartment on Norton Avenue, just north of Santa Monica Boulevard in West Hollywood, an enclave of unincorporated Los Angeles County completely surrounded by the city of Los Angeles. (West Hollywood became a two-square-mile refuge for homosexuals, since the Los Angeles County sheriff's deputies who patrolled the community were less authoritarian than their counterparts in the LAPD, and their patrols were less frequent. In 1984 West Hollywood was incorporated as an independent city.)

For a time, all was well. They bought pets—a dog and a small monkey. (California has since banned the keeping of monkeys as pets.) The animals soon became a point of contention, however. Tommy seemed jealous of the attention Doug gave them, especially the monkey.

Doug clearly did not share Tommy's passion for their partnership. "[It's not that] I *don't* love Tom, but I don't exactly *love* him either," he confided to a friend. Doug was also unhappy with Tommy's sex work, especially when Tommy brought clients home in the middle of the night. (In the *Advocate* article, Tommy is euphemistically referred to as "self-employed.")

Tommy was drinking heavily and possibly using drugs. An acquaintance recalled seeing Tommy staggering along a street in Hollywood, "bombed out of his mind on something."

Doug confided in a sixty-nine-year-old neighbor named Theta Rodman who lived a block away on Fountain Avenue. Doug and Theta had

---

* My account of Tommy and Doug's relationship is largely based on "Love and Violent Death in Hollywood" by Rob Cole and Pete Craig (Los Angeles *Advocate*, June 23–July 6, 1971); Tommy's autopsy report; and interviews with Tommy's friends. My request for the Los Angeles Police Department files on the case was denied because, under California law, "records of investigations conducted by, or investigatory files compiled by, any local police agency for law enforcement purposes are exempt from disclosure."

struck up an unlikely friendship based on their shared roots: they were both from Indiana. "He looked on me as a grandmother, though we aren't related," Rodman told the *Advocate*. "I just took a liking to him."

Tommy and Doug fought often, and violently. "He was a clothes tearer," an acquaintance said of Tommy. "He tore clothes off his lover's back, and he tore clothes off of other people. This was one of the ways he expressed his anger." Once when Doug was driving away after a fight, Tommy threw a rock through his windshield.

Whenever he and Tommy fought, Doug would seek refuge at Theta's. It was an incongruous scenario, the decorated war veteran seeking comfort and safety in the home of an aging widow. But Doug was increasingly running out of places where he felt safe. Tommy was fixated on Doug, addicted to alcohol and possibly drugs, and likely psychotic. Doug was still recovering from his tour in Vietnam and may have been suffering PTSD.

In mid-May 1971, Doug moved out of the Norton Avenue apartment, taking the dog and the monkey with him. First he moved into Theta's apartment, then he found a place of his own, an apartment at 6446 Lexington Avenue, just north of Santa Monica Boulevard in the heart of Hollywood. He shared the apartment with a friend named Rick Friedman, twenty-four, who later said he and Doug "were on the way to becoming lovers. It was more than just being roommates." By now Tommy was stalking Doug. Rick told Doug he'd noticed Tommy lurking around their apartment building one night. Doug said he was scared of Tommy. "I thought Doug was just being dramatic," Rick recalled.

On the afternoon of Tuesday, May 25, 1971, Doug and Rick were sitting around their apartment, discussing their future as a couple. "Doug thought he had finally got away from Tom. And he had found a new job," Rick remembered. "The last few days were the happiest in his life. He went about everywhere with a smile on his face." A little before seven that evening, Rick asked Doug if he wanted some beer. "Great," said Doug. Rick went out to get a six-pack.

Tommy was waiting outside the building. When Rick left, Tommy went inside to confront Doug. A few minutes after seven, Tommy kicked in the door to Doug's apartment. Neighbors heard screaming and yelling, and furniture breaking. A nurse who lived in the apartment next door ran onto her balcony to see Tommy and Doug struggling on Doug's balcony.

"My God!" Doug screamed at the nurse. "Call the cops, he's killing me!"

Frantically, the nurse went inside and dialed the nearest police station, the Hollywood Division, which was just a few blocks away. (Emergency 911 service would not be activated in California until 1972.) But the desk sergeant who answered her call seemed indifferent. The nurse described the struggle on the balcony. But the cop kept asking her if she'd actually witnessed a crime. Frustrated, the nurse hung up, and she and her roommate raced out of their apartment and into the hallway. They watched in horror as Doug staggered out of his apartment, bleeding profusely. He'd been stabbed once in the back. They reached him just as he collapsed down a flight of stairs. Behind them, Tommy emerged from Doug's apartment, holding a knife. He bolted down the stairs, chased by several neighbors, including an off-duty LAPD officer named David Berglund, who happened to live in the building.

Berglund chased Tommy into an alleyway behind the building and cornered him. He warned Tommy: "I've got a gun." Tommy didn't say anything. He just began stabbing himself in the stomach over and over while Berglund watched, shocked and speechless.

By now, after multiple calls from terrified neighbors, police had finally begun converging on the scene. But it was too late. Doug was dead on the stairs. Tommy was transported to the nearest hospital, where he died. According to the coroner's report, Tommy stabbed himself six times, piercing his liver, stomach, colon, and small intestine. He killed himself just four miles from the Ambassador Hotel, where Robert Kennedy had been assassinated three years earlier.

Doug Yeargin's family initially refused to claim his body. His father, Walter Yeargin Sr., told the coroner he didn't want it. Finally, Doug's friend Theta Rodman called the father. "Are you going to claim it?" she asked him angrily. She said the father eventually responded with a "weak yes." Doug's remains were cremated.

Tommy's family brought his body back to Evarts for burial. When word reached Evarts that Tommy had been stabbed to death, his friends naturally assumed he was murdered. Even today, some of them question the official account of his death, but it seems clear that Tommy killed himself. I had my own suspicions until I found the well-researched and well-reported article about the murder-suicide published in the Los Angeles *Advocate* shortly after the events unfolded.

I emailed the article to a few of Tommy's friends. "I really hated to hear such news about Tommy," wrote one in reply. "Altho had he lived he would have been almost seventy now, he will always be that young boy in my mind. Such a waste of brains and talent, but considering the violence his father showed his mother, it's little wonder that Tommy showed the same behaviors. He took it in with his mother's milk."

Part IV

After the Trip

Evarts High School closed in 2008. The building, shown here in July 2018, is now mostly vacant.
Author's photo

44

Another Thing
I Wish to Comment
on Is Your Long Hair

ON FRIDAY, FEBRUARY 16, 1968, two days after Kennedy left eastern Kentucky, a Democratic state senator named Edward Murphy rose to deliver a speech on the floor of the Kentucky Senate chamber at the State Capitol in Frankfort. Murphy attacked Kennedy for "blackening" Kentucky's image. He said Kennedy had put the state's "shame—and poverty and want . . . on display for all to see," and he invited Kennedy to return to Kentucky to "visit the thriving, industrious people on our farms and in our factories and our stores and our offices."

"I want the news media that follow him around to have a chance to show the world the other side of Kentucky's coin—the side that makes this the finest place in the world in which to live," Murphy said. "I have to wonder why—if this concern for the needy is motivated by anything other than a quest for votes—that this senator did not go among the poor who sent him to Washington—the poor of New York City." (Kennedy, of course, had spent considerable time touring the ghettos of New York.) Murphy also took a shot at the cost of the trip, saying he wanted to know "how many poor people could be fed for a month on what his recent trip to Kentucky cost the taxpayers."*

According to one report, Murphy's speech "drew heavy applause from the Senate."

At least one reporter who covered the trip came away convinced that Kennedy was serious about wanting to help the people of eastern Kentucky. The *Louisville Courier-Journal's* William Greider, who would go on to a long career in journalism and as of 2019 was a national affairs correspondent for the *Nation*, wrote a column about the trip that was published on February 18, 1968.

> The temptation is to be cynical, to write off the whole business of Kennedy touring Appalachia as a pose, an exercise in news making, a political happening.
>
> That, I must confess, was my first impression of the two-day tour but, at the end I came away convinced that Kennedy's interest was genuine and that in some small measure the people of the mountains may be better off because he came. . . .
>
> At several points, he literally had time only to pop in the door, ask the people if they were hungry, then run off. It was difficult to see how those interviews will contribute to the deliberations of the US Senate.
>
> Despite all this, despite the gimmicks, Kennedy's visit to the hollows and coal camps did have genuine meaning. At least, he convinced me.
>
> Hour after hour, he slogged from door to door with a persistence that exhausted and exasperated many of those who were following him.
>
> At each cabin he asked the same simple questions about how the people managed to live. While some of the conversations were banal and awkward, most of them were poignant.
>
> He was obviously deeply affected by what he saw and heard.

---

* By modern standards, at least, the cost of Kennedy's trip was surprisingly small. He and the two assistants who accompanied him flew commercial. A round-trip plane ticket from Washington to Lexington at the time cost about $65 (about $478 today). Kentucky governor Louie Nunn supplied a car and a state trooper to chauffeur Kennedy. And Alice Lloyd College hosted the small entourage overnight gratis.

Robert Kennedy received more mail by far than any other US senator, hundreds of letters a week, many of which are archived at his brother's presidential library in Boston. Reading the letters that Kennedy received in the winter of 1967–68 is a lot like listening to talk radio today, or scrolling through a combative Twitter feed. If you think political dialogue seems angry and mean today, take heart! It was just as bad—albeit eminently more literate—fifty years ago.

After his trip to Kentucky, Kennedy received a handful of letters thanking him for taking the time to investigate conditions there, including one from Clive Gordon Hall, a minister of the Old Regular Baptist Church in Dema, Kentucky. "The people here were thrilled to hear you speak at the Alice Lloyd College," Hall wrote in a neat cursive script. "You are the first official from outside our state who has cared enough for us to come and make a speech at the local college and to talk freely with the people about their problems." Hall ended his letter with a plea for donations of used clothing: "Many don't have enough clothes to keep them warm. If your family or friends have any clothing that they are considering discarding, I'm sure that someone here would be glad to have them."

But most of the letters Kennedy received after the trip were critical and often caustic.

> When you recently visited Kentucky you seemed surprised to hear that some Kentuckians on welfare were eating gravy and bread toward the end of the month. Senator, my husband, baby and I ate gravy, cornbread and beans for three years untill [sic] he passed his C.P.A. exam.
>
> Sometimes even now to save money we still eat gravy, cornbread and beans.
>
> You know what really burns me up? Is to check out at the grocery store behind someone with food stamps who has made a lot of silly purchases such as real butter, whipping cream (in the spray bomb), frozen dinners, instant potatoes, etc. While there I stand—a taxpayer—with my cart loaded down with dry

milk, potatoes, maragine [*sic*] and dream whip. And of course beans. . . .

Do you know we have families here in Kentucky in the third generation of welfare!

What has happen[ed] to pride in self, country and truth? If the welfare program needs more money, it is because the money now allocated isn't getting down thru the channels to the real needy.

—Mrs. Audrey Young, Elizabethtown, Kentucky

I saw you on Television the other evening, when you strut-[t]ed through Eastern Kentucky heaping insult upon misery. It so happens I was borned [*sic*] in Kentucky. . . .

Senator you have a lot to learn about people from Kentucky [and] other States in the South. They may be poor but, they are proud. There are ways of helping people without insulting them and when President Johnson traveled through those areas he did not strut into peoples [*sic*] homes and have a camera following him and ask them what they had for breakfast. I remember that we had many rough times when we were children but, we never accepted a cent of welfare in our life and if anyone had ever came into our home and ask us what we had for breakfast, I'm sure my Father would have thrown them out. . . .

Senator for a number of years you have been screaming about dignity for the Negro[e]s. Well you seem to have [a] different idea of dignity for white people. You would have spent your time much better, had you stayed in Washington and worked on the people who oppose the President's Legislature bills to help the very people you insulted.

I was pleased when one Gentleman told you they could not get their sons deferred from the draft because they did not have money to get the boys in college because I remember how you defended those Beatniks who call themselves Interlectuals [*sic*] to evade the draft.

—Elise Pays, St. Clair Shores, Michigan

Am getting sick and tired of you visiting the different states commenting on their poverty, your latest one being Ky. If you were half as well bred as the people in Ky. you would know how to conduct yourself and be more careful of your speeches. With all of your millions what in the world do you and your family know of poverty?

I think you would do better if you would stay home and look at your own state. What do you know of the conditions existing in other states? You would do well to let each one take care of their own people and government. After all you are traveling on the taxpayers' money which they don't appreciate.

Another thing I wish to comment on is your long hair. You are entirely too old to wear a beattle [*sic*] haircut. It would be much better if you would get a man's haircut which would make you look much better groomed.

I am so sick and tired of hearing you speak of your dead brother. Why don't you let him rest in peace, or are you using him as a means of getting votes, which would never sway me to even vote once for you. Your brother was certainly a gentleman and always well groomed.

Is it true that you once made the statement that you would like to give your blood to the Viet Cong, if so I am all for it—every drop of it.* Am sure your brother J.F.K. would not have approved of your statement. Why not give your blood to our American boys if you have it to spare. They are dying for all of us.

I don't think I will ever get an answer from you, but at least you know how I feel and many of my friends and their families feel the same way.

I love my good old U.S.A. and every thing in it and especially the stars and stripes in our flag.

—Mrs. F. M. DaCosta, Whitehaven, Tennessee

---

* At a November 1965 press conference, Kennedy said he was not opposed to the International Red Cross delivering to North Vietnam blood donated by Americans. "If we've given all the blood needed to the South Vietnamese," he said, "I'm willing to give blood to anybody who needs it." Conservatives considered the statement tantamount to treason.

45

I Knew Something Was Wrong

ON FEBRUARY 16, 1968, the same day the Kentucky state senator excoriated Kennedy for "blackening" Kentucky's image, Peter Edelman sent Kennedy a lengthy memo titled "Recommendations from Eastern Kentucky Trip." In it, Edelman proposed drastic changes in the federal food stamp and job training programs, as well as tax incentives for companies to move to the area. Specifically, Edelman wrote, "food stamp prices must be lowered."

> Our hearings in Kentucky revealed what we already knew from our hearings [in Mississippi] last year—that food stamp prices are too high. It is the continued belief of the committee staff that food stamps should be free to people with no income, and that the method of determining the normal expenditure for food of people whose incomes are below $200 a month is faulty.

Kennedy would have scant opportunity to act on Edelman's suggestions, of course, but over time, "EPR"—eliminate the purchase requirement for food stamps—became a rallying cry for antipoverty activists. The requirement was finally lifted by the Food Stamp Act of 1977, which took effect on January 1, 1979. Participation in the food stamp program increased by 1.5 million within a month.

Beginning in 1990, stamps were phased out and replaced with Electronic Benefit Transfer (EBT) cards—essentially debit cards that are attached to a recipient's benefits account. With stamps obsolete, the program was officially renamed the Supplemental Nutrition Assistance Program, or SNAP, in 2008.

Food stamps have become an essential program for the nation's poor. In fiscal year 2018, more than forty million Americans—more than 12 percent of the country's population—received SNAP benefits. On average, participants received $125.52 a month in assistance—a total of more than $60 billion.

Food stamps have also become an important source of income for the twenty-five thousand retailers nationwide that accept them. Although retailers are neither required nor inclined to reveal how much of their income comes from customers redeeming food stamps, the business consultancy AlixPartners estimates that the single largest beneficiary of this largesse is Walmart, where 18 percent of all SNAP benefits were redeemed in 2013 (the most recent year for which figures are available). That amounts to about $13 billion—roughly 4 percent of Walmart's total sales in the United States.

On Saturday, March 16, 1968, Robert Kennedy launched his presidential campaign. Fifteen days later, President Johnson shocked the nation by announcing he would not seek another term. Early on the morning of June 5, Kennedy was shot. Nell Meade Fields, who'd attended the hearing in Neon less than four months earlier, remembers hearing the news. "I remember getting off the school bus and I was walking to our home. We lived way up in the holler, and when we got close I seen my mother on the front porch and she was wavin' and hollerin' at us, and I knew something was wrong. I thought maybe somebody in the family had died, and when we got close she said they shot Bobby Kennedy. It had happened the night before, but we didn't hear about it until the next day. It was like seeing a family member had died."

Kennedy died on June 6, 1968.

Steve Cawood had just finished law school in May and was planning to go to work for the Kennedy campaign as soon as he passed the bar exam. The exam was scheduled for June 10, the Monday after Kennedy's assassination. "It was just devastating," Cawood tells me. "I took my bar and flunked it. My mind was gone."

Cawood passed the exam on his second try and became what his hero Harry Caudill had been, a small-town lawyer who specialized in representing "little people." Unlike Caudill, however, Cawood does not plan to live out his final days in eastern Kentucky. When I interviewed him in the summer of 2018, he and his wife, Sissy—they were married in 1966—were planning to leave Pineville to be closer to one of their daughters. "Our children were the first in my family that had to leave here because they didn't have a job—they weren't trained to do anything they could come back here and make a living with. One lives in Lexington and one lives in Chattanooga. My father's family were the first Europeans to settle Harlan County and my mother's family were the first to settle Leslie County. And my wife and I are fixin' to sell this home and move to Chattanooga because we don't have anybody here to care for us. And when I grew up, my grandmothers had to approve who I asked for a date because we were kin to so many people. Now neither one of us has any family here."

On November 5, 1968, five months after Kennedy was assassinated, Richard Nixon was elected president. Soon after taking office the following January, he appointed an obscure congressman from Illinois to head the Office of Economic Opportunity. That congressman, Donald Rumsfeld, would hire as one of his top assistants an ambitions congressional intern from Wyoming named Dick Cheney.

Together, Rumsfeld and Cheney would begin the long process of ending the War on Poverty. Over the next decade, the most successful antipoverty programs—Head Start and the school meal program among them—were transferred to other federal agencies, and in 1981 the Office of Economic Opportunity was finally abolished altogether.

In 2014 the *New York Times*' analytical unit, the Upshot, ranked each county in the nation based on six factors: educational attainment, household income, jobless rate, disability rate, life expectancy, and obesity rate. Six counties in eastern Kentucky—Breathitt, Clay, Jackson, Lee, Leslie, and Magoffin—ranked among the bottom ten. "Clay County, in dead last, might as well be in a different country," wrote Annie Lowrey in the *Times*.

> The median household income there is barely above the poverty line, at $22,296, and is just over half the nationwide median. Only 7.4 percent of the population has a bachelor's degree or higher. The unemployment rate is 12.7 percent. The disability rate is nearly as high, at 11.7 percent. (Nationwide, that figure is 1.3 percent.) Life expectancy is six years shorter than average. Perhaps related, nearly half of Clay County is obese.

46

Cote's Cemetery

On a muggy Saturday morning in July 2018, I meet Jeanette Zimek Knowles and Brenda Bailey Taylor in the parking lot of the Clover Fork Clinic, a community health care clinic in Evarts founded in 1970 and an enduring legacy of the War on Poverty. We are going to visit Tommy Duff's grave.

Jeanette, the AV in charge of the Cloverfork Youth Group, and Brenda, Tommy's high school friend and a member the youth group, have not visited Tommy's final resting place in decades. But first we take a brief tour of the town. Evarts High School, which is right next door to the clinic, closed in 2008, when three Harlan County high schools were merged into a single gleaming new Harlan County High School. Brenda, who graduated from Evarts High in 1969—soon after she got married—points out where the trailers that housed the hated "temporary" classrooms behind the building used to be. Brenda's family was poor, and she couldn't always afford to buy the required textbooks, so she had to take good notes in class. She'd collect broken pencils from the wastebaskets. When a teacher required all essays be written in ink, Brenda had to beg for a waiver: she didn't own a pen. (Her request was granted.)

Plans to redevelop the old Evarts High School have so far come to naught, and the building now stands mostly vacant. On the facade, the letters spelling EVARTS HIGH SCHOOL are still there, and I am pleased to see that the *S* in *SCHOOL* is no longer missing.

We walk across the street to Kilgores, a clothing store and five-and-dime that was a favorite haunt of students from Evarts High and is today something of a time capsule. Two small terriers greet us at the door. Boxes of shoes and Halloween costumes seemingly forty years old are stacked high on the shelves. The shopkeeper, Sidney Johnson, speaks with a thick Kentucky accent. When Jeanette asks her for directions to the cemetery, she apologizes for using "Colored Town" as a landmark. On the counter near the front of the store is an impressive collection of local history books. I buy one for fifteen dollars: *Taproots: A History of Cloverfork*, written by the 1987–88 Evarts High School humanities class. As we are leaving, Sidney asks me to let her know when my book comes out, because she might want to stock it. Brenda later tells me not to get my hopes up. She says Sidney is very picky about the books Kilgores sells. She reads them first and only sells the ones she really likes.

The three of us climb into my rental car and head east on KY 38 three or four miles to a small cemetery called Cote's—or Colt's, depending whom you ask. "Now don't get frisky," Brenda admonishes me when I begin driving a bit too fast on the narrow gravel road leading up the steep hill to the graves. We park in a small lot and begin searching for Tommy Duff's headstone. Mosquitos swarm around us. Sweat drips from the bill of my baseball cap.

After a few minutes, Brenda finds it on the hillside, engulfed in the kudzu that is overrunning the cemetery. She bends down to pull away the weeds and reveals the inscription etched into the big gray stone.

DUFF

THOMAS CLAUDE	OVA TINA
OCT. 1, 1949	FEB. 7, 1931
MAY 25, 1971	AUG. 9, 1976

TWAS GRACE THAT BROUGHT ME SAFE THUS FAR
AND GRACE THAT TOOK ME HOME.

The three of us stand in silence for a few moments. "Well, Tommy, we came to visit," Jeanette finally says. "You've been there a long time. Who knows what you'd be doing today if you were still here."

Tommy Duff's grave, Cote's Cemetery, Evarts, Kentucky. *Author's photo*

Acknowledgments

I AM INDEBTED TO THE PEOPLE OF EASTERN KENTUCKY who opened their hearts and homes to me and shared their memories of Robert Kennedy's visit and the tumultuous times in which it occurred. Their generosity was overwhelming. I am especially grateful to Lawrence Baldridge; Bonnie Carroll; Steve Cawood; Dee Davis; Cheryl, Michele, and Richetta Farris; Jeanette Zimek Knowles; and David Ledford.

Peter Edelman patiently answered my many questions, John Petersen read the manuscript and offered valuable suggestions, and Jeffrey Coleman supplied much-needed moral support.

The following institutions were most helpful: Dolph Briscoe Center for American History, University of Texas at Austin; John F. Kennedy Presidential Library and Museum, Boston, Massachusetts; Library of Congress, Washington, DC; Lyndon Baines Johnson Library and Museum, Austin, Texas; McGaw Library, Alice Lloyd College, Pippa Passes, Kentucky; and Special Collections & Archives, Berea College, Berea, Kentucky.

I have been blessed with an outstanding agent, Jane Dystel, and an outstanding editor, Jerry Pohlen, both of whom have encouraged and supported me for more than a decade now. I thank them both from the bottom of my heart.

Finally, and as always, I could achieve nothing worthwhile without the love and support of my wife, Allyson, and our daughter, Zaya. *Volim vas oboje.*

Sources

My account of Robert Kennedy's tour of Appalachia is based primarily on my interviews and correspondence with eyewitnesses to the trip, as well as contemporaneous newspaper accounts. I am indebted to the reporters who covered the tour, especially William Greider of the *Louisville Courier-Journal* and Pat Gish of the *Mountain Eagle* in Whitesburg. Their work in 1968 made mine fifty years later much easier.

A complete list of sources follows, but a few merit special recognition. The Robert F. Kennedy Papers at the JFK Library in Boston were a priceless resource, as were the oral histories in the Jo Zingg / Jeanette Knowles Appalachian Volunteers Oral History Collection at Berea College and the War on Poverty Oral History Project at the University of Kentucky's Louie B. Nunn Center for Oral History. I am deeply indebted to Cheryl, Michele, and Richetta Farris for making their grandmother Mary Rice Farris's papers available to me, including a copy of the speech she delivered at Berea College in October 1968; to Steve Gardner for allowing me access to Dave Zegeer's papers; and to Jeanette Knowles for providing me with copies of all the Cloverfork Youth Group newsletters. The transcripts of the hearings held in Vortex and Neon were indispensable, of course, as was the tape recording of Kennedy's remarks at Alice Lloyd College, generously provided to me by Bennie Moore.

Interviews & Correspondence

Lawrence Baldridge
Billy Dean Carroll
Bonnie Carroll
Jill Carson
Ron Carson
Steve Cawood
Roy Crawford
Dee Davis
Debbie Deal
Rebecca Draper
Peter Edelman
Cheryl Farris
Michele Farris
Richetta Farris
Nell Meade Fields
Oakley Fugate
J. Steven Gardner
Ben Gish
Larry Hayes
Loyal Jones
Jeanette Zimek Knowles

David Ledford
John Malpede
Al McSurely
Henrietta Tolliver Milich
Bennie L. Moore
Lou Murrey
Gary Parr
Mimi Pickering
Cathy Rasche
Mildred Shackleford
Robert Shaffer
Harvey Sloane
Taylor Smith
Brenda Bailey Taylor
Ethel Thornsberry
LRW
Lowell Wagner
Victor W. Weedn
Angie Willett
Thelma Witt

Contemporaneous Newspaper Coverage

Floyd County Times (Prestonsburg, KY)
Harlan (KY) Daily Enterprise
Hazard (KY) Herald
Kentucky Kernel (University of Kentucky student paper, Lexington, KY)
Lexington (KY) Herald
Lexington (KY) Leader

Louisville (KY) Courier-Journal
Louisville (KY) Times
Messenger-Inquirer (Owensboro, KY)
Mountain Eagle (Whitesburg, KY)
New York Times
Pike County News (Pikeville, KY)
Washington Post

Other Articles

Abdullah, F., A. Nuernberg, and R. Rabinovici. "Self-Inflicted Abdominal Stab Wounds." *Injury* 34, no. 1 (January 2003): 35–39.

Bedway, Barbara. "Even a Firebombing Didn't Stop This Legendary Publisher's 'Screams.'" *Editor & Publisher*, January 27, 2009.

Black, Kate, and Marc A. Rhorer. "Out in the Mountains: Exploring Lesbian and Gay Lives." *Journal of the Appalachian Studies Association* 7 (1995): 16–25.

Breed, Allen G. "Kentucky Man Weary of Media Attention." *Owensboro (KY) Messenger-Inquirer*, July 24, 1994.

Bristol (TN) News Bulletin. "Commissaries in Tennessee Are Planned." September 11, 1934.

Carey, Leigh Ann. "Raise Hell and Eat Cornbread, Comrades!" *Slate*, November 5, 2018.

Cassidy, Robert. "Stripping Out the Facts." *Louisville Courier-Journal*, April 23, 1972.

Chan, Sewell. "Mollie Orshansky, Statistician, Dies at 91." *New York Times*, April 17, 2007.

Clark, Krissy. "The Secret Life of a Food Stamp Might Become a Little Less Secret." *Slate*, August 5, 2014.

Cole, Rob, and Pete Craig. "Love and Violent Death in Hollywood." *Advocate* (Los Angeles), July 23, 1971.

Cooper, Bob. "'Outsiders,' Berea's Negroes Shake Sleepy Town." *Cincinnati Enquirer*, September 3, 1968.

Cornett, Alice. "The Sgt. York Syndrome." *Baltimore Sun*, November 11, 1991.

Elam, Constance. "Culture, Poverty and Education in Appalachian Kentucky." *Education and Culture* 18, no. 1 (Spring 2002): 10–13.

Elmira (NY) Star-Gazette. "Food Stamp Test Begins." May 16, 1939.

Fenton, John H. "Goldwater Hits Johnson Speech." *New York Times*, January 9, 1964.

Fisher, Gordon M. "The Development and History of the Poverty Thresholds." *Social Security Bulletin* 55, no. 4 (Winter 1992): 3–14.

Fleming, John. "The Death of Willie Brewster: Memories of a Dark Time." *Anniston (AL) Star*, March 22, 2009.

Fossett, Katelyn. "Black Appalachia." *Politico Magazine*, June 22, 2017.

Gabriel, Trip. "50 Years into the War on Poverty, Hardship Hits Back." *New York Times*, April 20, 2014.

Hampson, Rick. "RFK's Visit to Appalachia, 50 Years Later: How Kennedy Country Became Trump Country." *USA Today*, February 12, 2018.

Hopcraft, David. "Dayton Men to Blame, Says Berea Mayor After Shootout." *Dayton (OH) Journal Herald*, September 3, 1968.

Howard, Christopher, Amirio Freeman, April Wilson, and Eboni Brown. "The Polls—Trends: Poverty." *Public Opinion Quarterly* 81, no. 3 (Fall 2017): 769–789.

Hutton, Bob. "Hillbilly Elitism." *Jacobin Magazine*, October 1, 2016.

Ingram, Bob. "Wallace Partisans Elated as Lurleen Enters Race." *Montgomery (AL) Advertiser*, February 25, 1966.

Johnson, Oakley. "Starvation and the Reds in Kentucky." *Nation*, February 3, 1932.

Jones, Sarah. "J.D. Vance, the False Prophet of Blue America." *New Republic*, November 17, 2016.

Kiffmeyer, Thomas. "From Self-Help to Sedition: The Appalachian Volunteers in Eastern Kentucky, 1964–1970." *Journal of Southern History* 64, no. 1 (February 1998): 65–94.

Kocher, Greg. "Coal Magnate Bill Sturgill, UK Benefactor and Former Chairman of Its Board, Dies at 89." *Lexington (KY) Herald-Leader*, July 20, 2014.

Lemann, Nicholas. "The Realpolitik RFK." *Washington Post*, May 23, 1993.

Levin, Josh. "The Welfare Queen." *Slate*, December 19, 2013.

Louisville Courier-Journal. "Governor Flays Bill He Signed." March 26, 1920.

Lovan, Dylan. "Few Mountaintop Removal Sites Reclaimed After Mining." *Nashville (TN) Tennessean*, December 30, 2010.

Lowrey, Annie. "What's the Matter with Eastern Kentucky?" *New York Times Magazine*, June 26, 2014.

Luigart, Fred, Jr. "Compassion for a Region." *Louisville Courier-Journal*, July 7, 1963.

Mai-Duc, Christine. "The 'Angry Man's Candidate': George Wallace and the Roots of the American Independent Party." *Los Angeles Times*, April 17, 2016.

McCullough, David. "The Lonely War of a Good Angry Man." *American Heritage*, December 1969.

Merriam, C. E., Jr. "Thomas Paine's Political Theories." *Political Science Quarterly* 14, no. 3 (September 1899): 389–403.

Nevin, David. "These Murdered Old Mountains." *Life*, January 12, 1968.

New York Daily News. "18 Anti-Bobby Pickets Jailed in Montgomery." April 26, 1963.

New York Times. "Grocers Approve Plan to Aid Needy." March 14, 1939.

———. "234,600 Hogs for Needy." December 31, 1933.

Ockerman, Emma. "African Americans in Appalachia Fight to Be Seen as a Part of Coal Country." *Washington Post*, August 10, 2017.

Orshansky, Mollie. "Children of the Poor." *Social Security Bulletin* 26, no. 7 (July 1963): 3–13.

Owensboro (KY) Messenger. "Harlan Disorders Are Blamed on the National Miners Union and Red Cross." December 8, 1931.

———. "Unemployed Union Miners Ready to 'Help Themselves.'" May 14, 1931.

Pearce, John Ed. "Symbol of Controversy." *Courier-Journal & Times Magazine*, February 7, 1971.

Pericak, Andrew A., Christian J. Thomas, David A. Kroodsma, Matthew F. Wasson, Matthew R. V. Ross, Nicholas E. Clinton, David J. Campagna, Yolandita Franklin, Emily S. Bernhardt, and John F. Amos. "Mapping the Yearly Extent of Surface Coal Mining in Central Appalachia Using Landsat and Google Earth Engine." Edited by Juan A. Añel. *PLOS ONE* 13, no. 7 (July 25, 2018): e0197758. https://doi.org/10.1371/journal.pone.0197758.

Pfister, Tom. "Gaining Ground from Reclaimed Abandoned Mine Lands." *Forbes*, September 3, 2018.

Puckett, Anita. "On the Pronunciation of Appalachia." *Now & Then*, Summer 2000.

Quisenberry, A. C. "Kentuckians in the Battle of Lake Erie." *Register of Kentucky State Historical Society* 9, no. 27 (September 1911): 41, 43–49.

Roysdon, Keith, and Robin Gibson. "'River' of Immigrants from the South Shaped Muncie." *Muncie (IN) Star Press*, August 23, 2014.

Ryperson, Sylvia, and Judah Schept. "Building Prisons in Appalachia." *Boston Review*, April 28, 2018.

Schwartzman, Paul. "They Were Kentucky's Poorest, Most Desperate People. And He Was a Kennedy with an Entourage." *Washington Post*, February 21, 2018.

Selma (AL) Times-Journal. "Governor Has Cancer." June 27, 1967.

Southern Cross (Chu Lai, Vietnam). "Soldier Earns Bronze and Silver Stars." October 22, 1969.

Sullivan, Mark. "Stamps for Needy to Get Surplus Food Questioned." *Philadelphia Inquirer*, May 9, 1939.

Swanson, Doug J. "Symbol of War on Poverty a Sign of Program Failures." *Owensboro (KY) Messenger-Inquirer*, June 12, 1992.

Tampa (FL) Times. "Alabama Steady Without 'Captain.'" February 9, 1968.

Trillin, Calvin. "The Logical Thing, Costwise." *New Yorker*, December 27, 1969.

———. "A Stranger with a Camera." *New Yorker*, April 12, 1969.

Vance, Kyle. "Can Strip-Mine Spoil Banks Be a Green Bonanza?" *Louisville Courier-Journal*, July 26, 1964.

———. "3 Sedition Cases in Pike Are Sent to Grand Jury." *Louisville Courier-Journal*, August 19, 1967.

Voskuhl, John. "Whitesburg: Sophisticated and Down-Home in the Shadow of Pine Mountain." *Louisville Courier-Journal*, July 29, 1991.

Wahba, Phil. "Walmart Could Lose $12.7 Billion in Sales Over Next Decade If Food Stamps Are Slashed." *Fortune*, June 30, 2017.

Walker, Don. "Berea Council, Citizens Seeking to Allay Unrest." *Louisville Courier-Journal*, September 3, 1968.

Wilkerson, Jessica. "Unraveling the Hidden Black History of Appalachian Activism." *Salon*, August 3, 2018.

Wilkes-Barre (PA) Times Leader Evening News. "Food Stamps Load Family Dinner Table." September 12, 1939.

Zeitz, Joshua. "What Everyone Gets Wrong About LBJ's Great Society." *Politico Magazine*, January 28, 2018.

Books & Other Sources

Alderman, Ellen, and Caroline Kennedy. *In Our Defense: The Bill of Rights in Action*. New York: Morrow, 1991.

Atkins, Leah Rawls. *John M. Harbert III: Marching to the Beat of a Different Drummer*. Birmingham, AL: Tarva House, 1999.

Bageant, Joe. *Deer Hunting with Jesus: Dispatches from America's Class War*. New York: Crown, 2008.

Barrett, Elizabeth, dir. *Stranger with a Camera*. Season 13 of *POV*. PBS, July 11, 2000.

Bhatraju, Kiran. *Mud Creek Medicine: The Life of Eula Hall and the Fight for Appalachia*. Louisville, KY: Butler Books, 2013.

Bowden, Mark. *Huế 1968: A Turning Point of the American War in Vietnam*. New York: Atlantic Monthly Press, 2017.

Carter, Dan T. *The Politics of Rage: George Wallace, the Origins of the New Conservatism, and the Transformation of American Politics*. Baton Rouge: Louisiana State University Press, 2000.

Catte, Elizabeth. *What You Are Getting Wrong About Appalachia*. Cleveland, OH: Belt, 2018.

Caudill, Harry M. Letter to William Shockley, August 26, 1974. University of
    Kentucky Special Collections Library. Via Internet Archive, https://archive
    .org/details/516209-caudill-8-26-74.

———. *Night Comes to the Cumberlands: A Biography of a Depressed Area.*
    Ashland, KY: Jesse Stuart Foundation, 2001.

Cheves, John, Bill Estep, and Linda Blackford. *Fifty Years of Night.* Lexington,
    KY: Lexington Herald-Leader, 2014.

Clark, Thomas D. *A History of Kentucky.* Ashland, KY: Jesse Stuart Founda-
    tion, 1988.

Clinton, Hillary Rodham. *What Happened.* New York: Simon & Schuster, 2017.

Council of Economic Advisers. *The War on Poverty 50 Years Later: A Progress
    Report.* Council of Economic Advisers, January 2014.

Darraj, Susan Muaddi. *John F. Kennedy.* Philadelphia: Chelsea House, 2004.

David, Lester, and Irene David. *Bobby Kennedy: The Making of a Folk Hero.*
    New York: Dodd, Mead, 1986.

Dooley, Brian. *Robert Kennedy: The Final Years.* New York: St. Martin's, 1996.

Dreiser, Theodore, and National Committee for the Defense of Political Prison-
    ers, eds. *Harlan Miners Speak: Report on Terrorism in the Kentucky Coal
    Fields.* Lexington: University Press of Kentucky, 2008.

Edelman, Peter B. *Searching for America's Heart: RFK and the Renewal of Hope.*
    Boston: Houghton Mifflin, 2001.

———. *So Rich, So Poor: Why It's So Hard to End Poverty in America.* New
    York: New Press, 2013.

Eller, Ronald D. *Uneven Ground: Appalachia Since 1945.* Lexington: University
    Press of Kentucky, 2013.

Evarts High School Humanities Class. *Taproots: A History of Cloverfork.* Evarts,
    KY: Shoestring Press, 1988.

Faderman, Lillian, and Stuart Timmons. *Gay L.A.: A History of Sexual Outlaws,
    Power Politics, and Lipstick Lesbians.* New York: Basic Books, 2006.

Farley, William. "A Stubborn Courage: Mean and Ornery Journalists in Eastern
    Kentucky." PhD diss., University of Kentucky, 2017.

Fetterman, John. *Stinking Creek.* New York: Dutton, 1967.

Food and Nutrition Service, US Department of Agriculture. "A Short History
    of SNAP." Accessed August 19, 2019. https://www.fns.usda.gov/snap/short
    -history-snap.

Ford, Thomas R. *Health and Demography in Kentucky.* Lexington: University
    of Kentucky Press, 1964.

———, ed. *The Southern Appalachian Region: A Survey*. Lexington: University of Kentucky Press, 1962.

Freese, Barbara. *Coal: A Human History*. New York: Penguin Books, 2004.

Hall, Wade H., ed. *The Kentucky Anthology: Two Hundred Years of Writing in the Bluegrass State*. Lexington: University Press of Kentucky, 2005.

Harrington, Michael. *The Other America: Poverty in the United States*. New York: Penguin Books, 1992.

Harris, Richard. *Freedom Spent: Tales of Tyranny in America*. Boston: Little, Brown, 1976.

Hayes, Stephen F. *Cheney: The Untold Story of America's Most Powerful and Controversial Vice President*. New York: HarperCollins, 2007.

Hevener, John W. *Which Side Are You On? The Harlan County Coal Miners, 1931–39*. Urbana: University of Illinois Press, 1978.

Hoerr, John P. *And the Wolf Finally Came: The Decline of the American Steel Industry*. Pittsburgh: University of Pittsburgh Press, 1988.

Isenberg, Nancy. *White Trash: The 400-Year Untold History of Class in America*. New York: Viking, 2016.

Katz, Michael B. *In the Shadow of the Poorhouse: A Social History of Welfare in America*. New York: Basic Books, 1986.

Kennedy, Robert F. *RFK: His Words for Our Times*. Edited by C. Richard Allen and Edwin O. Guthman. New York: William Morrow, 2018.

Kiffmeyer, Thomas. *Reformers to Radicals: The Appalachian Volunteers and the War on Poverty*. Lexington: University Press of Kentucky, 2009.

King, Martin Luther, Jr. *Where Do We Go from Here: Chaos or Community?* New York: Harper & Row, 1967.

Kurlansky, Mark. *1968: The Year That Rocked the World*. New York: Random House, 2005.

Lesher, Stephan. *George Wallace: American Populist*. Reading, MA: Addison-Wesley, 1994.

Lewis, Ronald L., Jennifer Egolf, Ken Fones-Wolf, and Louis C. Martin, eds. *Culture, Class, and Politics in Modern Appalachia: Essays in Honor of Ronald L. Lewis*. Morgantown: West Virginia University Press, 2009.

Malpede, John. The Robert F. Kennedy Performance Project. Accessed January 28, 2019. http://rfkineky.org/.

Montrie, Chad. *To Save the Land and the People: A History of Opposition to Surface Coal Mining in Appalachia*. Chapel Hill: University of North Carolina Press, 2003.

Moynihan, Daniel P. *The Politics of a Guaranteed Income: The Nixon Administration and the Family Assistance Plan.* New York: Random House, 1973.

Nelson, Craig. *Thomas Paine: Enlightenment, Revolution, and the Birth of Modern Nations.* New York: Viking, 2006.

Noble, Golden. *True Story of the Life & Experiences of a One-Room School Teacher.* Hazard, KY: Self-published, 2011.

Palermo, Joseph A. *In His Own Right: The Political Odyssey of Senator Robert F. Kennedy.* New York: Columbia University Press, 2002.

Pimpare, Stephen. *A People's History of Poverty in America.* New York: New Press, 2008.

Portelli, Alessandro. *They Say in Harlan County: An Oral History.* New York: Oxford University Press, 2011.

Reece, Erik. *Lost Mountain: A Year in the Vanishing Wilderness; Radical Strip Mining and the Devastation of Appalachia.* New York: Riverhead Books, 2006.

Rumsfeld, Donald. *Known and Unknown: A Memoir.* New York: Sentinel, 2011.

Schlesinger, Arthur M. *Robert Kennedy and His Times.* Boston: Houghton Mifflin, 1978.

Schmitt, Edward R. *President of the Other America: Robert Kennedy and the Politics of Poverty.* Amherst: University of Massachusetts Press, 2011.

Schultz, Bud, and Ruth Schultz. *It Did Happen Here: Recollections of Political Repression in America.* Berkeley: University of California Press, 1989.

Scott, Rebecca R. *Removing Mountains: Extracting Nature and Identity in the Appalachian Coalfields.* Minneapolis: University of Minnesota Press, 2010.

Searles, P. David. *A College for Appalachia: Alice Lloyd on Caney Creek.* Lexington: University Press of Kentucky, 1995.

Steel, Ronald. *In Love with Night: The American Romance with Robert Kennedy.* New York: Simon & Schuster, 2000.

Stewart, Bruce E., ed. *Blood in the Hills: A History of Violence in Appalachia.* Lexington: University Press of Kentucky, 2012.

Stoll, Steven. *Ramp Hollow: The Ordeal of Appalachia.* New York: Hill and Wang, 2017.

Theobald, Robert, ed. *The Guaranteed Income: Next Step in Economic Evolution?* Garden City, NY: Doubleday, 1966.

Thomas, Evan. *Robert Kennedy: His Life.* New York: Simon & Schuster, 2000.

Trattner, Walter I. *From Poor Law to Welfare State: A History of Social Welfare in America.* New York: Free Press, 1994.

Turner, William Hobart, and Edward J. Cabbell, eds. *Blacks in Appalachia.* Lexington: University Press of Kentucky, 1985.

Tye, Larry. *Bobby Kennedy: The Making of a Liberal Icon*. New York: Random House, 2016.

US House of Representatives Committee on Un-American Activities. *Guide to Subversive Organizations and Publications*. Washington, DC: US Government Printing Office, 1961.

US Senate Subcommittee on Employment, Manpower, and Poverty. "Field Hearings—Eastern Kentucky." Transcript of hearing held at Neon, KY, February 14, 1968. http://rfkineky.org/docs/Neon_transcript.pdf.

———. "Field Hearings—Eastern Kentucky." Transcript of hearing held at Vortex, KY, February 13, 1968. http://rfkineky.org/docs/Vortex_transcript.pdf.

Walker, Don. *Modernizing the Mountaineer: People, Power, and Planning in Appalachia*. Knoxville: University of Tennessee Press, 1994.

Walls, David S., and John B. Stephenson. *Appalachia in the Sixties: Decade of Reawakening*. Lexington: University Press of Kentucky, 1972.

Webb, Clive. *Rabble Rousers: The American Far Right in the Civil Rights Era*. Athens: University of Georgia Press, 2010.

Whilden, Blakely Elizabeth. "Mineral Rights in Central Appalachia: A Brief History of the Broad Form Deed in Kentucky and Tennessee." University of North Carolina School of Law, accessed August 19, 2019. http://studentorgs.law.unc.edu/documents/elp/2012/whilden_final.pdf.

Whisnant, David E. *All That Is Native & Fine: The Politics of Culture in an American Region*. Chapel Hill: University of North Carolina Press, 1988.

Wilkerson, Jessica. *To Live Here, You Have to Fight: How Women Led Appalachian Movements for Social Justice*. Urbana: University of Illinois Press, 2018.

———. "Where Movements Meet: From the War on Poverty to Grassroots Feminism in the Appalachian South." PhD diss., University of North Carolina, 2014.

Williams, Daniel K. *Defenders of the Unborn: The Pro-Life Movement Before Roe v. Wade*. New York: Oxford University Press, 2016.

Witcover, Jules. *85 Days: The Last Campaign of Robert Kennedy*. New York: Quill, 1988.

Yang, Andrew. *The War on Normal People: The Truth About America's Disappearing Jobs and Why Universal Basic Income Is Our Future*. New York: Hachette Books, 2018.

Zegeer, David, and Shannon Lamkin. *Inside MSHA: The Formative Years of the Mine Safety and Health Administration*. Edited by J. Steven Gardner. Lexington: Kentucky Foundation, 2014.

Index

Page numbers in italics indicate illustrations